Python and AWS Cookbook

Mitch Garnaat

Beijing · Cambridge · Farnham · Köln · Sebastopol · Tokyo

Python and AWS Cookbook

by Mitch Garnaat

Published by O'Reilly Media, Inc., 1005 Gravenstein Highway North, Sebastopol, CA 95472.

O'Reilly books may be purchased for educational, business, or sales promotional use. Online editions are also available for most titles (*http://my.safaribooksonline.com*). For more information, contact our corporate/institutional sales department: (800) 998-9938 or *corporate@oreilly.com*.

Editors: Julie Steele and Meghan Blanchette	**Cover Designer:** Karen Montgomery
Production Editor: Teresa Elsey	**Interior Designer:** David Futato
	Illustrator: Robert Romano

Revision History for the First Edition:

2011-10-21   First release

See *http://oreilly.com/catalog/errata.csp?isbn=9781449305444* for release details.

ISBN: 978-1-449-30544-4

[LSI]

1319206006

Table of Contents

Preface

My first experience with Amazon Web Services was on March 14, 2006. I had seen a press release announcing a new web-based storage service called Simple Storage Service (S3), and I remember thinking how strange it seemed that Amazon would be offering such a service. Nevertheless, I signed up for an account and started reading the documentation.

I was blown away by S3. The simple, affordable pricing model. The elegant REST API. The virtually unlimited storage capacity. Amazing. The only thing that could make this any better, I thought to myself, would be a Python interface! That day I started coding what would become the boto (*https://github.com/boto/boto*) library, which is what we will use in this book to interface with Amazon Web Services.

I still believe that Python is a great language for interacting with AWS and other cloud services. The fantastic standard libraries that come with all Python installations (Batteries Included!), the vast collection of modules available for quick download via the Python Cheese Shop (*http://pypi.python.org/*), and the ability to work interactively with cloud services, trying requests and immediately seeing the results, combine to provide a powerful and fun way to develop applications and control your cloud-based infrastructure.

I've always found that the best way to learn something new is to see lots of examples. That's what this little book will focus on: solutions to many common problems related to EC2 and S3 (using Python and boto). I hope you find it useful!

Conventions Used in This Book

The following typographical conventions are used in this book:

Italic
: Indicates new terms, URLs, email addresses, filenames, and file extensions.

`Constant width`
: Used for program listings, as well as within paragraphs to refer to program elements such as variable or function names, databases, data types, environment variables, statements, and keywords.

Constant width bold
> Shows commands or other text that should be typed literally by the user.

Constant width italic
> Shows text that should be replaced with user-supplied values or by values determined by context.

This icon signifies a tip, suggestion, or general note.

This icon indicates a warning or caution.

Using Code Examples

This book is here to help you get your job done. In general, you may use the code in this book in your programs and documentation. You do not need to contact us for permission unless you're reproducing a significant portion of the code. For example, writing a program that uses several chunks of code from this book does not require permission. Selling or distributing a CD-ROM of examples from O'Reilly books does require permission. Answering a question by citing this book and quoting example code does not require permission. Incorporating a significant amount of example code from this book into your product's documentation does require permission.

We appreciate, but do not require, attribution. An attribution usually includes the title, author, publisher, and ISBN. For example: "*Python and AWS Cookbook* by Mitch Garnaat (O'Reilly). Copyright 2012 Mitch Garnaat, 978-1-449-30544-4."

If you feel your use of code examples falls outside fair use or the permission given above, feel free to contact us at *permissions@oreilly.com*.

Safari® Books Online

  Safari Books Online is an on-demand digital library that lets you easily search over 7,500 technology and creative reference books and videos to find the answers you need quickly.

With a subscription, you can read any page and watch any video from our library online. Read books on your cell phone and mobile devices. Access new titles before they are available for print, and get exclusive access to manuscripts in development and post feedback for the authors. Copy and paste code samples, organize your favorites, download chapters, bookmark key sections, create notes, print out pages, and benefit from tons of other time-saving features.

O'Reilly Media has uploaded this book to the Safari Books Online service. To have full digital access to this book and others on similar topics from O'Reilly and other publishers, sign up for free at *http://my.safaribooksonline.com*.

How to Contact Us

Please address comments and questions concerning this book to the publisher:

O'Reilly Media, Inc.
1005 Gravenstein Highway North
Sebastopol, CA 95472
800-998-9938 (in the United States or Canada)
707-829-0515 (international or local)
707-829-0104 (fax)

We have a web page for this book, where we list errata, examples, and any additional information. You can access this page at:

http://shop.oreilly.com/product/0636920020202.do

To comment or ask technical questions about this book, send email to:

bookquestions@oreilly.com

For more information about our books, courses, conferences, and news, see our website at *http://www.oreilly.com*.

Find us on Facebook: *http://facebook.com/oreilly*

Follow us on Twitter: *http://twitter.com/oreillymedia*

Watch us on YouTube: *http://www.youtube.com/oreillymedia*

## CHAPTER 1

General Info

1.1 A Quick Note About Python

The examples in this book use Python 2.7.1, although they should work with any version of Python from 2.5.x to 2.7.x. The boto library has not yet been ported and fully tested on Python 3.x, although there are plans to do so in the near future.

All versions of Python, in both source form and precompiled for many popular platforms, can be found at *http://python.org*.

1.2 Installing boto

The examples in this book require boto version 2.1 or later. There are several options available to you when it comes to installing boto.

Download and Install from github.com

The boto project uses github (*http://github.com*) as its source code repository. You can clone our github repo locally and install boto from that cloned distribution. By doing so, you will always have access to the very latest changes in boto. That includes the newest features, as well as the newest bugs, so you will have to decide if this intrepid path is for you or not:

```
% git clone https://github.com/boto/boto
% cd boto
% sudo python setup.py install
```

Manually Download and Install boto

The Python Cheese Shop (*http://pypi.python.org/*) is the official repository of Python packages. If you go to the Cheese Shop (also known as PyPI) and search for boto, you will see a page like Figure 1-1, although it should be for version 2.1, not 2.0.

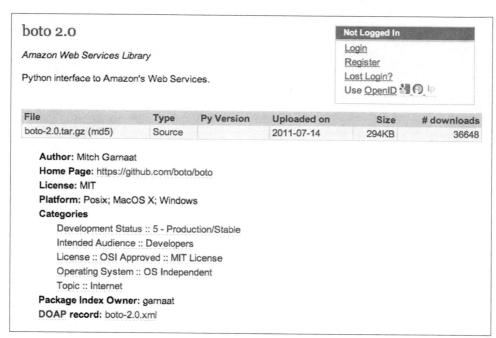

Figure 1-1. boto Page on PyPI

Clicking on the *boto-2.1.tar.gz* link will download the compressed tarball containing the source package for boto. Save this file on your local machine and follow this process to install from the source package:

```
% tar xfz boto-2.1.tar.gz
% cd boto-2.1
% sudo python setup.py install
```

Installing boto with easy_install

The easy_install utility makes it easy (of course!) to find, install, upgrade, and uninstall Python packages. Before you can use the nice features of easy_install, you first need to, erm, install it. Detailed instructions for installing the setuptools package (of which easy_install is part) can be found at *http://pypi.python.org/pypi/setuptools*. Many Linux distributions also have packages for setuptools. For example, on Ubuntu, you can do this:

```
% sudo apt-get install python-setuptools
```

On yum-based distros such as Fedora and CentOS, you can do:

```
% sudo yum install python-setuptools
```

Once you have easy_install set up on your machine, installing boto is easy:

```
% sudo easy_install boto
```

Installing boto with pip

The pip utility is another tool to find, install, upgrade, and uninstall Python packages. In my experience, both work well, so do a bit of research and make up your own mind. Or use both! Detailed instructions for installing pip can be found at *http://pypi.python .org/pypi/pip*. Once you have pip set up on your machine, installing boto is similarly easy:

```
% sudo pip install boto
```

Installing boto with virtualenv

One final option in the litany of installation options is actually not an installation tool at all, but a very handy way of creating isolated Python environments. With virtua lenv you can create any number of isolated, self-contained Python environments on your workstation. Packages that are installed in these virtual environments will not affect your system Python packages or other virtual environments. I have found this is a very useful way to have many different projects in progress on my laptop without worrying about changes or mistakes in one project affecting other projects or my global environment. As an added benefit, once you have installed virtualenv and created an environment, you automatically have access to both easy_install and pip within those environments and installing software within the environment does not require super-user or administrator rights.

Detailed instructions for installing virtualenv can be found at *http://pypi.python.org/ pypi/virtualenv*. Once you have virtualenv set up on your machine, you can set up a virtual environment:

```
% virtualenv paws
```

You can name your virtualenv whatever you like, obviously. You can then enable your virtual environment and install boto:

```
% cd paws
% source bin/activate
% pip install boto
```

Installing paramiko

The paramiko package implements the SSH2 protocol for secure connections to remote machines. You can use boto without paramiko, but some of the EC2 recipes in this book depend on the paramiko package, so I would recommend installing it. You can manually install it using the instructions on *http://www.lag.net/paramiko/*, or, if you have installed easy_install or pip, you can do easy_install paramiko or pip install paramiko.

Installing euca2ools

One final package you might want to install is euca2ools. This package was developed by the Eucalyptus team to provide command-line tools that are compatible with the tools supplied by AWS. euca2ools is written in Python and built on top of boto. It provides a great set of tools to help you manage your cloud infrastructure as well as providing good example code to study and extend.

euca2ools has been packaged by many Linux distros. On Ubuntu, you can install it via sudo apt-get -y euca2ools. On yum-based distros, you can do sudo yum install euca2ools. You can also get the latest version of the source code at *https://launchpad .net/euca2ools* or download packaged source releases from *http://open.eucalyptus.com/ downloads*.

1.3 Getting Started with Amazon Web Services

Create Your AWS Account

The first thing you will need to do to use Amazon Web Services is sign up for an account. Go to *http://aws.amazon.com/* and click on the Sign Up Now button. If you already have an account with Amazon.com and want to associate your AWS activity with that account, you can simply log in with those credentials. If you prefer, you can create a new account just for your AWS activity.

For detailed instructions on signing up for AWS, you can check out this tutorial (*http: //support.rightscale.com/1._Tutorials/01-RightScale/1.5_Sign-up_for_AWS*), provided by RightScale (*http://rightscale.com*).

Make sure your account has been enabled for at least the EC2 service and the S3 service. The tutorial linked to above provides detailed instructions on signing up for services.

Once your account has been created, a variety of credentials will be associated with it:

AWS Account Credentials
> These are the credentials you use to log into the AWS web portal and the AWS Management Console and consist of an email address and a password. Since these credentials control access to all of the other credentials discussed below, it is very important to choose a strong password for this account and to age the password aggressively.

AWS Account Number
> This is the unique 12-digit number associated with your AWS account. Unlike the other credentials we will discuss, this one is not a secret. The easiest way to find your account number is to look in the upper-right corner of the web page after you have logged into the AWS portal. You should see something like Figure 1-2.

> The Account Number is a public identifier and is used mainly for sharing resources within AWS. For example, if I create an AMI in EC2 and I want to share that AMI with a specific user without making the AMI public, I would need to add that user's Account Number to the list of user IDs associated with the AMI. One potential source of confusion here: even though the Account Number is displayed with

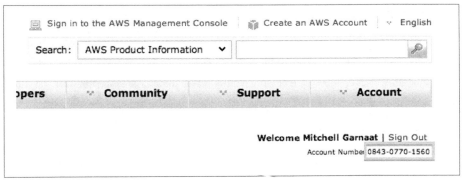

Figure 1-2. Finding Your AWS Account Number

hyphens separating the three groups of four digits, when it is used via the API, the hyphens must be removed.

AccessKeyID and SecretAccessKey

These Access Identifiers are at the heart of all API access in AWS. Every REST or Query API request made to every AWS service requires you to pass your AccessKeyID to identify who you are. The APIs also require you to compute and include a *signature* in the request.

The *signature* is calculated by concatenating a number of elements of the request (e.g., timestamp, request name, parameters, etc.) into a StringToSign and then creating a *signature* by computing an HMAC of the StringToSign using your SecretAccessKey as the key.

When the request is received by AWS, the service concatenates the same String-ToSign and then computes the *signature* based on the SecretAccessKey AWS has associated with the AccessKeyID sent in the request. If they match, the request is authenticated. If not, it is rejected.

The AccessKeyID associated with an account cannot be changed, but the SecretAccessKey can be regenerated at any time using the AWS portal. Because the SecretAccessKey is the shared secret upon which the entire authentication mechanism is based, if there is any risk that your SecretAccessKey has been compromised, you should regenerate it.

X.509 Certificate

The other Access Identifier associated with your account is the X.509 Certificate. You can provide your own certificate or you can have AWS generate a certificate for you. This certificate can be used for authenticating requests when using the SOAP versions of the AWS APIs, and it is also used when creating your own S3-based AMIs in EC2. Essentially, the files that are created when bundling an AMI are cryptographically signed using the X.509 cert associated with your account, so if anyone were to try to tamper with the bundled AMI, the signature would be broken and easily detected.

When using the SOAP APIs, the X.509 certificate is as critically important from a security point of view as the SecretAccessKey discussed above, and it should be managed just as carefully. Remember, even if you don't use SOAP, a hacker could!

SSH Keys

The final credential we need to discuss is the public/private keypair used for SSH access to an EC2 instance. By default, an EC2 instance will allow SSH access only by PublicKey authentication. I strongly recommend that you stick to this policy in any AMIs you create for your own use. SSH keypairs can be generated via the AWS Console and API, or you can import existing keypairs. You should create keypairs for each individual in your organization that will need access to running instances and guard those SSH keys carefully.

Managing Your AWS Credentials in boto

Once you have signed up for your AWS account and obtained your credentials, you need to make boto aware of them. There are several ways to do this:

Explicitly pass credentials to boto

Each time you want to access some AWS service, you need to create a connection to that service with boto. At that time, you can pass in your access key ID and secret access key explicitly and boto will use those credentials when communicating with the service:

```
% python
Python 2.7.1 (r271:86882M, Nov 30 2010, 10:35:34)
[GCC 4.2.1 (Apple Inc. build 5664)] on darwin
Type "help", "copyright", "credits" or "license" for more information.
>>> import boto
>>> ec2 = boto.connect_ec2(aws_access_key_id='my_access_key',
aws_secret_access_key='my_secret_key')
```

Most people find that this gets tedious pretty quickly.

Store credentials in environment variables

If no explicit credentials are passed to boto when making a connection (as shown above), boto will look to see if the environment variables AWS_ACCESS_KEY_ID and AWS_SECRET_ACCESS_KEY are defined in the user's environment. If they are, boto will use the values of these environment variables as the access key and secret key.

Store credentials in the boto config file

If boto doesn't get credentials passed to it explicitly and it doesn't find them in the user's environment, it will try to find them in the boto configuration files. By default, boto will look for configuration information in */etc/boto.cfg* and in *~/.boto*. If you want to store your config info elsewhere, you can set the environment variable BOTO_CONFIG to the path to the config file and boto will read it from there. To add your credentials to the boto config file, you would add a section like this:

```
[Credentials]
aws_access_key_id = your_access_key
aws_secret_access_key = your_secret_key
```

Once the credentials are stored in the boto config file, boto will use them automatically each time you use it. This is the most convenient way to deal with your AWS credentials. However, if you store your AWS credentials in your boto config file, you should set the file protections such that the file is readable only by you.

A Quick Test

Hopefully, at this point you have boto installed and you have your AWS account created and your credentials stored in environment variables or the boto config file. Before moving on, let's just do a quick test to verify that things are working:

```
% python
Python 2.7.1 (r271:86882M, Nov 30 2010, 10:35:34)
[GCC 4.2.1 (Apple Inc. build 5664)] on darwin
Type "help", "copyright", "credits" or "license" for more information.
>>> import boto
>>> ec2 = boto.connect_ec2()
>>> ec2.get_all_zones()
[Zone:us-east-1a, Zone:us-east-1b, Zone:us-east-1c, Zone:us-east-1d]
>>>
```

If you get roughly the same output when you run this little test, you should be all set to proceed with the recipes. If not, double-check the previous steps. If you are still stuck, try posting a question on the boto users group (*http://groups.google.com/group/ boto-users*).

1.4 Using boto with Eucalyptus

What Is Eucalyptus?

From *http://open.eucalyptus.com/learn/what-is-eucalyptus*:

> Eucalyptus enables the creation of on-premise private clouds, with no requirements for retooling the organization's existing IT infrastructure or need to introduce specialized hardware. Eucalyptus implements an IaaS (Infrastructure as a Service) private cloud that is accessible via an API compatible with Amazon EC2 and Amazon S3. This compatibility allows any Eucalyptus cloud to be turned into a hybrid cloud, capable of drawing compute resources from public cloud. And Eucalyptus is compatible with a wealth of tools and applications that also adhere to the de facto EC2 and S3 standards.

In a nutshell, Eucalyptus allows you to set up your own AWS compatible mini-cloud (or maxi-cloud if you have enough hardware). Almost all of the recipes in this book for AWS will also work with Eucalyptus, so if you have some hardware, you can try all of this out without leaving the comfort and safety of your own network.

Getting and Installing Eucalyptus

For those interested in installing Eucalyptus, you might want to give the FastStart (*http://open.eucalyptus.com/try/faststart*) a try. FastStart is a way to get Eucalyptus up and running quickly with as few steps as possible.

Using the Eucalyptus Community Cloud

You can also try out Eucalyptus without installing any software at all. Eucalyptus provides a sandbox hosted environment called the Eucalyptus Community Cloud, where you can test-drive and experiment with Eucalyptus cloud software. For more information, visit *http://open.eucalyptus.com/try/community-cloud*.

Managing Your Eucalyptus Credentials in boto

Once you have Eucalyptus up and running, boto makes it easy to connect to the system. First, you can edit your boto config file to include your Eucalyptus hostname and credentials:

```
[Credentials]
euca_access_key_id = your_euca_access_key
euca_secret_access_key = your_euca_secret_key

[Boto]
eucalyptus_host = "DNS name or IP address of your Eucalyptus CLC"
walrus_host = "DNS name or IP address of your Walrus"
```

Once the information is entered into your boto config file, you can connect to Eucalyptus (the EC2-compatible service) and Walrus (the S3-compatible service) like this:

```
% python
>>> import boto
>>> euca = boto.connect_euca()
>>> walrus = boto.connect_walrus()
```

1.5 Using boto with Google Cloud Storage

What Is Google Cloud Storage?

Google Cloud Storage for Developers (*http://code.google.com/apis/storage/*) is a RESTful service for storing and accessing your data in Google's infrastructure. While Google Cloud Storage and S3 each offer some unique features of their own, they also have quite a bit of overlap both in functionality and in base API. Google developers have contributed significantly to boto to allow full access to Google Cloud Storage functionality in boto. Many of the S3 recipes in this book will also work on Google Cloud Storage.

Managing Your Google Cloud Storage Credentials in boto

Since Google Cloud Storage is a separate service, it has its own set of credentials. You can add these credentials to your boto config file like this:

```
[Credentials]
gs_access_key_id = your_gs_access_key
gs_secret_access_key = your_gs_secret_key
```

You can then create a connection to Google Cloud Storage:

```
% python
Python 2.7.1 (r271:86882M, Nov 30 2010, 10:35:34)
[GCC 4.2.1 (Apple Inc. build 5664)] on darwin
Type "help", "copyright", "credits" or "license" for more information.
>>> import boto
>>> gs = boto.connect_gs()
```

1.6 Finding Available Regions for AWS

By default, when you create a connection to the EC2 service in boto, it connects to the US-EAST-1 region. Originally, that was the only region available, but AWS has expanded its operations considerably and, at the time of this writing, EC2 was available in the following regions, each with its own endpoint:

- us-east-1 [US-East (Northern Virginia)]
- us-west-1 [US-West (Northern California)]
- eu-west-1 [EU (Ireland)]
- ap-southeast-1 [Asia Pacific (Singapore)]
- ap-northeast-1 [Asia Pacific (Tokyo)]

boto provides a number of ways to find and connect to these regions. For example, the following will return a list of all RegionInfo objects for a given service (EC2 in this case). Each of those RegionInfo objects has a connect method, which will return a Connection object for that region:

```
$ python
Python 2.7.1 (r271:86882M, Nov 30 2010, 10:35:34)
[GCC 4.2.1 (Apple Inc. build 5664)] on darwin
Type "help", "copyright", "credits" or "license" for more information.
>>> import boto.ec2
>>> boto.ec2.regions()
[RegionInfo:eu-west-1, RegionInfo:us-east-1, RegionInfo:ap-northeast-1,
RegionInfo:us-west-1, RegionInfo:ap-southeast-1]
>>> eu_conn = _[0].connect()
```

If you have the name of the region you want to connect to, you can also use this approach:

```
$ python
Python 2.7.1 (r271:86882M, Nov 30 2010, 10:35:34)
```

```
[GCC 4.2.1 (Apple Inc. build 5664)] on darwin
Type "help", "copyright", "credits" or "license" for more information.
>>> import boto.ec2
>>> eu_conn = boto.ec2.connect_to_region('eu-west-1')
>>>
```

Finally, if you would like to change the default region boto uses when creating an EC2 connection, you can do so by adding something like this to your boto config file:

```
[Boto]
ec2_region_name = eu-west-1
```

Once this has been added to your boto config file, when you call boto.connect_ec2 without any parameters you will get a connection to the eu-west-1 region.

1.7 Enabling Debug Output with boto

Occasionally, things don't work exactly as you expected. When you are interacting with remote services via HTTP-based APIs, the best debugging tool you can have is detailed logs of the actual HTTP requests and responses sent to and received from the remote services.

boto provides a way to get very detailed logging by using the Python logging module. Full details of the capabilities of the Python logging module can be found at *http://docs .python.org/library/logging.html*, but this example shows a quick way to get full debug output printed to your interactive console when using boto:

```
% python
>>> import boto
>>> boto.set_stream_logger('paws')
>>> ec2 = boto.connect_ec2(debug=2)
>>> s3 = boto.connect_s3(debug=2)
>>>
```

The string passed to set_stream_logger can be anything you want; it will appear in the header of log entries. Any operations performed with the ec2 or s3 connections from this point forward will dump full debug logs out to the interactive Python shell.

1.8 Controlling Socket Timeouts in boto

All of the APIs that boto uses to communicate with cloud services are HTTP-based. That means that under the covers we are communicating over sockets to distributed services. Sometimes these services can be unresponsive or the communication layer between our application and the service can be unreliable. To help manage this in a reasonable way, timeouts are important. They allow our application to detect a problem with the network or a service and attempt to deal with it, or at least tell the user about it.

You can explicitly manage socket-level `timeouts` in `boto` by adding a section to your boto config file. The `timeout` is specified in seconds:

```
[Boto]
http_socket_timeout = 5
```

## CHAPTER 2

EC2 Recipes

2.1 Launching an Instance

Problem

One of the first things most people want to do after they get signed up with AWS is to launch an instance.

Solution

Create the necessary prerequisite resources and then use the `run_instances` method to create an instance.

Discussion

If you are launching an instance, most likely you will want to log in to that instance once it is up and running. In the interest of security, AWS uses passwordless SSH for instance access. This requires the use of a public/private keypair that is used to control access to your instance. The public key is installed on the newly launched instance by EC2 and registered as an authorized key with the SSH software on the instance. Then, when you log into the instance, you provide the private key and the SSH software is able to cryptographically compare the public and private keys and determine if the login attempt should be allowed or not. So, prior to running our first instance, we need to create an SSH keypair.

In addition to the keypair, we also need to create a security group. Security groups are a distributed firewall used to control access to your instances. By default, all ports on your instance will be disabled so no access would be possible. If we want to access the instance via SSH, we need to create a security group that contains a specific rule that will enable access to the instance on the specific port we want to use for SSH (default is 22).

Example 2-1 shows a convenience function that does all of the hard work related to launching an instance.

Example 2-1. Launching an Instance

```
import os
import time
import boto
import boto.manage.cmdshell

def launch_instance(ami='ami-7341831a',
                     instance_type='t1.micro',
                     key_name='paws',
                     key_extension='.pem',
                     key_dir='~/.ssh',
                     group_name='paws',
                     ssh_port=22,
                     cidr='0.0.0.0/0',
                     tag='paws',
                     user_data=None,
                     cmd_shell=True,
                     login_user='ec2-user',
                     ssh_passwd=None):
    """
    Launch an instance and wait for it to start running.
    Returns a tuple consisting of the Instance object and the CmdShell
    object, if request, or None.

    ami        The ID of the Amazon Machine Image that this instance will
               be based on.  Default is a 64-bit Amazon Linux EBS image.

    instance_type The type of the instance.

    key_name   The name of the SSH Key used for logging into the instance.
               It will be created if it does not exist.

    key_extension The file extension for SSH private key files.

    key_dir    The path to the directory containing SSH private keys.
               This is usually ~/.ssh.

    group_name The name of the security group used to control access
               to the instance.  It will be created if it does not exist.

    ssh_port   The port number you want to use for SSH access (default 22).

    cidr       The CIDR block used to limit access to your instance.

    tag        A name that will be used to tag the instance so we can
               easily find it later.

    user_data  Data that will be passed to the newly started
               instance at launch and will be accessible via
               the metadata service running at http://169.254.169.254.

    cmd_shell  If true, a boto CmdShell object will be created and returned.
               This allows programmatic SSH access to the new instance.

    login_user The user name used when SSH'ing into new instance.  The
```

```
                default is 'ec2-user'

ssh_passwd  The password for your SSH key if it is encrypted with a
            passphrase.
"""
cmd = None

# Create a connection to EC2 service.
# You can pass credentials in to the connect_ec2 method explicitly
# or you can use the default credentials in your ~/.boto config file
# as we are doing here.
ec2 = boto.connect_ec2()

# Check to see if specified keypair already exists.
# If we get an InvalidKeyPair.NotFound error back from EC2,
# it means that it doesn't exist and we need to create it.
try:
    key = ec2.get_all_key_pairs(keynames=[key_name])[0]
except ec2.ResponseError, e:
    if e.code == 'InvalidKeyPair.NotFound':
        print 'Creating keypair: %s' % key_name
        # Create an SSH key to use when logging into instances.
        key = ec2.create_key_pair(key_name)

        # AWS will store the public key but the private key is
        # generated and returned and needs to be stored locally.
        # The save method will also chmod the file to protect
        # your private key.
        key.save(key_dir)
    else:
        raise

# Check to see if specified security group already exists.
# If we get an InvalidGroup.NotFound error back from EC2,
# it means that it doesn't exist and we need to create it.
try:
    group = ec2.get_all_security_groups(groupnames=[group_name])[0]
except ec2.ResponseError, e:
    if e.code == 'InvalidGroup.NotFound':
        print 'Creating Security Group: %s' % group_name
        # Create a security group to control access to instance via SSH.
        group = ec2.create_security_group(group_name,
                               'A group that allows SSH access')
    else:
        raise

# Add a rule to the security group to authorize SSH traffic
# on the specified port.
try:
    group.authorize('tcp', ssh_port, ssh_port, cidr)
except ec2.ResponseError, e:
    if e.code == 'InvalidPermission.Duplicate':
        print 'Security Group: %s already authorized' % group_name
    else:
        raise
```

```
# Now start up the instance.  The run_instances method
# has many, many parameters but these are all we need
# for now.
reservation = ec2.run_instances(ami,
                                 key_name=key_name,
                                 security_groups=[group_name],
                                 instance_type=instance_type,
                                 user_data=user_data)

# Find the actual Instance object inside the Reservation object
# returned by EC2.

instance = reservation.instances[0]

# The instance has been launched but it's not yet up and
# running.  Let's wait for its state to change to 'running'.

print 'waiting for instance'
while instance.state != 'running':
    print '.'
    time.sleep(5)
    instance.update()
print 'done'

# Let's tag the instance with the specified label so we can
# identify it later.
instance.add_tag(tag)

# The instance is now running, let's try to programmatically
# SSH to the instance using Paramiko via boto CmdShell.

if cmd_shell:
    key_path = os.path.join(os.path.expanduser(key_dir),
                            key_name+key_extension)
    cmd = boto.manage.cmdshell.sshclient_from_instance(instance,
                                                       key_path,
                                                       user_name=login_user)

return (instance, cmd)
```

Example 2-2 shows an example of an interactive Python session that uses the launch_instance function.

Example 2-2. Using the launch_instance Function

```
>>> from ec2_launch_instance import launch_instance
>>> launch_instance() ❶
Creating keypair: paws
Security Group: paws already authorized
waiting for instance
.
.
done
SSH Connection refused, will retry in 5 seconds
```

```
(Instance:i-98847ef8, <boto.manage.cmdshell.SSHClient object at 0x10141fb90>)
>>> instance, cmdshell = _ ❷
>>> cmdshell.shell() ❸

     _|  _|_  )
    _| (    /   Amazon Linux AMI
   __|\__|__|

See /usr/share/doc/system-release/ for latest release notes.
No packages needed for security; 1 packages available
[ec2-user@domU-12-31-39-00-E4-53 ~]$ ls
[ec2-user@domU-12-31-39-00-E4-53 ~]$ pwd
/home/ec2-user
[ec2-user@domU-12-31-39-00-E4-53 ~]$ df
Filesystem           1K-blocks     Used Available Use% Mounted on
/dev/xvda1            8256952    918228   7254864  12% /
tmpfs                 305624         0    305624   0% /dev/shm
[ec2-user@domU-12-31-39-00-E4-53 ~]$ ❹
[ec2-user@domU-12-31-39-00-E4-53 ~]$ logout

*** EOF
>>>
```

❶ Launch an instance with all of the default choices.

❷ The launch_instance function returns a tuple consisting of the Instance object and the CmdShell object. This line uses the special Python shell symbol _, which represents the last returned value to unpack the two values in the tuple into their own variables.

❸ The CmdShell object represents an SSH connection to our new instance. Here, we use the shell method to start up an interactive command shell to our new instance.

❹ Typing exit into the SSH session will close the interactive SSH session and return us to our Python prompt. You could now call instance.terminate() to get rid of the instance, or you can keep it around for more experimentation.

2.2 Keeping Track of Instances with Tags

Problem

As you create more instances, it becomes difficult to keep track of them.

Solution

Use the create_tag method and variants to associate meaningful tags with your EC2 resources.

Discussion

In Recipe 2.1 we created a single instance, and when there is only one, it's not that hard to keep track of it. As soon as you begin to create additional instances, however, things get more complicated—and by the time you have dozens or even hundreds of instances running at the same time, it's almost impossible to keep track of them all. Trying to remember what instance i-28a64341 is doing is hard, but if you can associate meaningful names with the instances, things become much more manageable.

The create_tags method gives us a way to associate keys or key/value pairs with EC2 resources. We can then use those tags to help filter results and find the resources we are looking for quickly and easily.

Example 2-3. Keeping Track of Instances with Tags

```
import boto

ec2 = boto.connect_ec2()

# Get a list of all current instances.  We will assume that the only
# instance running is the one we started in the previous recipe.

reservations = ec2.get_all_instances()

# Despite the name, get_all_instances does not return Instance
# objects directly.  What it returns are Reservation objects
# as returned by run_instances.  This is a confusing aspect of
# the EC2 API that we have decided to be consistent with in boto.
# The following incantation will return the actual Instance
# object embedded within the Reservation.  We are assuming we
# have a single Reservation which launched a single Instance.

instance = reservations[0].instances[0]

# We could call create_tags directly here but boto provides
# some nice convenience methods to make it even easier.
# We are going to store a single tag on this instance.

instance.add_tag('paws')

# We can now ask for all instances that have the tag name "paws"
# and get our instance back again.

reservations = ec2.get_all_instances(filters={'paws' : None})
new_instance = reservations[0].instances[0]
assert new_instance.id == instance.id
```

2.3 Accessing the Console Log

Problem

A recently launched instance is not behaving as you expected.

Solution

Use the `get_console_output` method to view the console log of the instance to trouble-shoot the problem.

Discussion

If you launch a new instance and are unable to log in, or if the instance doesn't seem to be performing as expected, one critical source of debugging information is the system log, the information that is printed out to the console as you are booting the machine. If the machine in question is sitting on your desktop, it's easy to get access to this, but if it's a virtualized machine somewhere in the cloud, additional tools are required.

The `get_console_output` method gives us a way to get at that console output via the EC2 API.

Example 2-4. Accessing the Console Output

```
import boto

ec2 = boto.connect_ec2()

# Let's assume the instance we are interested in has already been started
# in the previous examples and is tagged with "paws".  This little
# incantation will retrieve it for us.

instance = ec2.get_all_instances(filters={'paws' : None})[0].instances[0]
co = instance.get_console_output()
print co.output
```

2.4 Uploading Your Own SSH Keypair

Problem

You have an existing SSH keypair and you would prefer to use that for accessing instances rather than create a new keypair.

Solution

Use the `import_key_pair` method to upload the public key portion of your existing key to AWS.

Discussion

As we demonstrated in Recipe 2.1, it is easy to create a new SSH keypair for use when logging into your instances. However, you probably already have a number of SSH keypairs, and you may prefer to use one of those.

The `import_key_pair` method gives you a way to upload the public part of your keypair to EC2. When you do that, you assign a name to the keypair, and after that you can use it exactly like the keypairs you create with the `create_key_pair` method.

If you have an existing PEM-format keypair file, as generated by EC2 and other tools, you first need to extract the public key portion from the keypair file. You can use the `ssh-keygen` command that is part of the `OpenSSL` package to do this. Assume that your PEM files are located in ~/.ssh/:

```
% cd ~/.ssh
% ssh-keygen -e -f mykey.pem > mykey.pub
```

Example 2-5. Upload SSH Keypair

```
import boto

ec2 = boto.connect_ec2()

# Read the public key material from the file
fp = open('mykey.pub')
material = fp.read()
fp.close()
key_pair = ec2.import_key_pair('mykey', material)
```

2.5 Synchronizing SSH Keypairs Across EC2 Regions

Problem

You have created a keypair in one EC2 region and you would like to use the same keypair in other regions.

Solution

Use the `import_key_pair` method to upload the public key portion of your existing key to each region.

Discussion

EC2 regions are completely independent, and resources like keypairs created in one region are not accessible in other regions. If you want to have the same keypair available in multiple regions, you can use a technique similar to that used in Recipe 2.4 to copy the same keypair across multiple EC2 regions, as shown in Example 2-6. Make sure you have generated the public key file from your *.pem* file first.

Example 2-6. Upload SSH Keypair

```
import boto.ec2

def sync_keypairs(keypair_name, public_key_file):
    """
    Synchronize SSH keypairs across all EC2 regions.

    keypair_name      The name of the keypair.
    public_key_file   The path to the file containing the
                      public key portion of the keypair.
    """
    fp = open(public_key_file)
    material = fp.read()
    fp.close()

    for region in boto.ec2.regions():
        ec2 = region.connect()
        # Try to list the keypair.  If it doesn't exist
        # in this region, then import it.
        try:
            key = ec2.get_all_key_pairs(keynames=[keypair_name])[0]
            print 'Keypair(%s) already exists in %s' % (keypair_name,
                                                        region.name)
        except ec2.ResponseError, e:
            if e.code == 'InvalidKeyPair.NotFound':
                print 'Importing keypair(%s) to %s' % (keypair_name,
                                                       region.name)
                ec2.import_key_pair(keypair_name, material)
```

2.6 Associate an Elastic IP Address with an Instance

Problem

You would like to have a stable IP address to use to refer to an instance rather than the dynamically generated address used by default.

Solution

Use the allocate_address method to get an Elastic IP address and the asso ciate_address method to pair it with your instance.

Discussion

Each time you start up an instance, a new IP address is allocated to that instance. This is fine if you are just experimenting with AWS or if the instance works behind the scenes and never needs to be accessed by end users or other systems. But if the instance is a front-end web server, for example, this can be an issue, because if that instance fails for some reason or needs to be replaced with an instance with updated software, you will need to update your DNS records with the new IP address. Since DNS changes can take time to propagate and can be incorrectly cached by clients, this could cause a disruption to your service.

In AWS, the solution to this problem is the rather confusingly named Elastic IP Address. At least it's confusing to me, because it's really what most people would call a static IP address, and that doesn't seem all that elastic to me. You can easily associate it with any instance you want, however, so perhaps that's where the elasticity comes in. Using Elastic IP Addresses is a two-step process. First you have to allocate an IP address. Then, you associate that IP address with an instance. There is no charge for an Elastic IP Address that is being used, but if you allocate one and don't have it associated with an instance, there is a small, per-hour charge to discourage people from hoarding those valuable IP addresses.

Example 2-7. Associate Elastic IP Address with an Instance

```
import boto

ec2 = boto.connect_ec2()

# Let's assume the instance we are interested in has already been started
# in the previous examples and is tagged with "paws".  This little
# incantation will retrieve it for us.

instance = ec2.get_all_instances(filters={'paws' : None})[0].instances[0]

# Allocate an Elastic IP Address.  This will be associated with your
# account until you explicitly release it.

address = ec2.allocate_address()

# Associate our new Elastic IP Address with our instance.

ec2.associate_address(instance.id, address.public_ip)

# Alternatively, you could do this.

instance.use_ip(address)
```

2.7 Attach a Persistent EBS Volume to an Instance

Problem

You are storing data on an EC2 instance and you would like that data to persist even if the instance fails.

Solution

Use the create_volume method and other EBS-related methods to create a volume and attach it to an existing instance.

Discussion

All EC2 instances have a root volume associated with them. This is where the operating system is installed. The size of this root volume depends on how the image was bundled and whether the corresponding AMI is S3-backed or EBS-backed.

In addition, all EC2 instance types except the t1.micro have dedicated instance storage. The number of volumes and total amount of instance storage varies depending on the instance type, but all instance storage has one property in common: it is ephemeral. When you terminate the instance (or when it fails for some reason), all of the instance storage goes away and anything you have stored there will be lost.

To provide persistent storage (that is, storage that exists independent of an instance), EC2 provides Elastic Block Storage (EBS). EBS allows you to create volumes of any size (from 1 GB to 1 TB) and attach the volumes to any EC2 instance. If that instance fails for any reason, the volume can be reattached to a replacement instance and the data will then be available to that new instance.

EBS volumes have about the same reliability you would expect from a RAID device, so while failures are not common, they can happen. We will discuss ways to back up your EBS volume in Recipe 2.8.

Example 2-8. Attach a Volume

```python
import boto
import time

def create_and_attach_volume(instance, volume_size, device_name):
    """
    Create a new EBS volume and attach it to the instance.

    instance    The instance object representing the instance to which
                the volume will be attached.

    volume_size The size (in GB) of the new volume.

    device_name The device name to which the new volume will be
                referred to on the instance.
    """
    ec2 = instance.connection
    # Determine the Availability Zone of the instance
    azone = instance.placement

    volume = ec2.create_volume(volume_size, azone)

    # Wait for the volume to be created.
    while volume.status != 'available':
        time.sleep(5)
        volume.update()

    volume.attach(instance.id, device_name)
    return volume
```

2.8 Back Up Your EBS Volumes

Problem

You have vital information stored on EBS volumes and you want to make sure that the data is safe.

Solution

Use the `create_snapshot` method and other EBS-related methods to back up your EBS volume and manage the backups.

Discussion

In Recipe 2.7 we discussed the reliability of EBS volumes, but no matter how reliable they may be, you still want to make sure you have a good backup strategy. That's where *snapshots* come in. A snapshot allows you to make a copy of your EBS volume at an instant in time and save that data to S3, with the whole 11 nines of durability that it provides.

Example 2-9. Snapshot an EBS Volume

```
>>> import boto
>>> ec2 = boto.connect_ec2()
>>> reservations = ec2.get_all_instances(filters={'paws' : None})
>>> instance = reservations[0].instances[0] ❶
>>> volumes = ec2.get_all_volumes(filters={'attachment.instance-id' : instance.id})
>>> volumes
[Volume:vol-990e5af3, Volume:vol-bdf7a2d7] ❷
>>> for v in volumes:
....:    print v.attach_data.device
....:
/dev/sdh ❸
/dev/sda1
>>> snaps = [v.create_snapshot() for v in volumes] ❹
>>> snaps
[Snapshot:snap-42a60b21, Snapshot:snap-40a60b23]
>>>
```

❶ Find the instance whose volumes we want to snapshot. This assumes it is the instance we started in an earlier recipe and is tagged with the label paws.

❷ Even though we have attached only one EBS volume to this instance, our query returns two volumes. That's because this is an EBS-backed AMI and one of those volumes represents the root volume of the instance.

❸ We can loop through each of the volumes to print out the device name associated with each to determine which is the root volume.

❹ Use a list comprehension in Python to create a list of snapshots, one for each volume.

The snapshot command makes a copy of the state of the volume at an instant in time. It's up to you to make sure that it's the *right* instant in time. For example, if you have a database that is writing data to the volume, you may need to temporarily halt the database so you get consistent information on the volume at the time you perform the snapshot. Some people format their volumes with xfs file system and then freeze the file system before running the snapshot and unfreeze immediately after. The details of all of this are very application-specific, but it's important to validate the integrity of your backups by restoring some snapshots (as shown in Recipe 2.9) and testing them.

2.9 Restore a Volume from a Snapshot

Problem

An EBS volume fails and you need to recover from a snapshot.

Solution

Use the `create_volume` method to create a new EBS volume from an existing snapshot.

Discussion

If you have been regularly creating snapshots of your EBS volumes, you will be well-prepared for the failure that will inevitably occur. And failure really is inevitable. Plan for it. That's not a criticism of cloud computing; it's just a fact of life. The good news is that the APIs that are available in cloud computing environments like AWS and Eucalyptus make it possible to automate the recovery of anticipated failures.

This recipe assumes that you have already identified the EBS volume that needs to be recovered and shows the simple steps required to create a new volume based on the latest snapshot of the failing volume.

Did you know that frequent snapshots will actually reduce the chances that your EBS volume will fail? It's true! The chance of failure increases as the amount of data since your last snapshot grows. Taking frequent snapshots can keep the amount of changed data smaller and increase the overall durability of your EBS volume.

Example 2-10. Restoring an EBS Volume

```
>>> import boto
>>> ec2 = boto.connect_ec2()
>>> volume_id = 'vol-bdf7a2d7' # The failing EBS volume
>>> bad_volume = ec2.get_all_volumes([volume_id])[0]
>>> snaps = bad_volume.snapshots() ❶
>>> snaps.sort(key=lambda snap: snap.start_time) ❷
```

```
>>> latest_snap = snaps[-1]  ❸
>>> new_volume = ec2.create_volume(bad_volume.size, bad_volume.zone, latest_snap)  ❹
```

❶ The snapshots method returns a list of snapshots for the volume.

❷ This example assumes you want the latest snapshot, so we sort the list by the start_time attribute.

❸ Once sorted, the latest snapshot should be the last one in the list.

❹ We now create a new volume, the same size as the bad volume and in the same availability zone as the bad volume, and based on the latest snapshot.

2.10 Clone an Existing Instance

Problem

You have a running instance, perhaps with EBS volumes attached, and you want to make a clone of that instance.

Solution

Use the get_userdata and clone_instance functions in this recipe to create a copy of an existing instance, including copies of all attached EBS volumes based on the latest available snapshots.

Discussion

For this recipe, let's assume that you have a running instance. It could have one or more EBS volumes attached to it. Let's also assume that, for some reason, you want to create another instance that is an exact copy of the currently running instance. You may want to do this because the running instance appears to be having issues or it may be that you want to debug an issue without disturbing your production instance.

Whatever the reason may be, this recipe defines a function to help us clone a running instance. To accomplish this, we need to gather some information:

- We need to know the AMI, keypair, security groups, availability zone, instance type, etc. of the current instance. We can get all of that information easily from the boto Instance object that represents the current instance.

- We need to make copies of all EBS volumes that are attached to the instance. For this recipe, we will assume that the latest snapshot of the volumes represents the state we want to recreate.

- We need the user_data that was passed to the instance when it was started. This data could include data and/or scripts that are run when the instance is launched as shown in Recipe 2.15.

Example 2-11. Clone a Running Instance

```python
import boto
from boto.ec2.blockdevicemapping import BlockDeviceMapping, BlockDeviceType
import os
import base64

def clone_instance(instance):
    """
    Make an clone of an existing Instance object.

    instance        The Instance object to clone.
    """
    new_bdm = None
    ec2 = instance.connection

    if instance.block_device_mapping:
        root_device_name = instance.get_attribute('rootDeviceName')['rootDeviceName']
        user_data = instance.get_attribute('userData')['userData']
        # user_data comes back base64 encoded.  Need to decode it so it
        # can get re-encoded by run_instance !
        user_data = base64.b64decode(user_data)
        new_bdm = BlockDeviceMapping()
        for dev in instance.block_device_mapping:
            # if this entry is about the root device, skip it
            if dev != root_device_name:
                bdt = instance.block_device_mapping[dev]
                if bdt.volume_id:
                    volume = ec2.get_all_volumes([bdt.volume_id])[0]
                    snaps = volume.snapshots()
                    if len(snaps) == 0:
                        print 'No snapshots available for %s' % volume.id
                    else:
                        # sort the list of snapshots, newest is at the end now
                        snaps.sort(key=lambda snap: snap.start_time)
                        latest_snap = snaps[-1]
                        new_bdt = BlockDeviceType()
                        new_bdt.snapshot_id = latest_snap.id
                        new_bdm[dev] = new_bdt

    return ec2.run_instances(instance.image_id,
                        key_name=instance.key_name,
                        security_groups=[g.name for g in instance.groups],
                        user_data=user_data,
                        instance_type=instance.instance_type,
                        kernel_id=instance.kernel,
                        ramdisk_id=instance.ramdisk,
                        monitoring_enabled=instance.monitored,
                        placement=instance.placement,
                        block_device_map=new_bdm).instances[0]
```

2.11 Find All Running EC2 Instances

Problem

There are now multiple EC2 regions spread across the world. In addition, you may have multiple accounts that you manage (for dev, test, production, etc.). Given that, it is easy to lose track of instances. And even though you may have forgotten about them, AWS has not, and you will continue to incur charges for these forgotten resources.

Solution

Use the EC2 API to find all running instances, for one or more accounts across all regions.

Discussion

Fortunately, the EC2 API makes it relatively easy to find all running instances, for all accounts, across all regions. Example 2-12 gathers all of that information together and prints a report, and also returns a data structure that can be used to terminate unused instances.

Example 2-12. Find All Running Instances

```python
import boto
import boto.ec2

def print_running_instances(running_instances):
    print 'The following running instances were found'
    for account_name in running_instances:
        print '\tAccount: %s' % account_name
        d = running_instances[account_name]
        for region_name in d:
            print '\t\tRegion: %s' % region_name
            for instance in d[region_name]:
                print '\t\t\tAn %s instance: %s' % (instance.instance_type,
                                                    instance.id)
                print '\t\t\t\tTags=%s' % instance.tags

def find_all_running_instances(accounts=None, quiet=False):
    """
    Will find all running instances across all EC2 regions for all of the
    accounts supplied.

    :type accounts: dict
    :param accounts: A dictionary contain account information.  The key is
                     a string identifying the account (e.g. "dev") and the
                     value is a tuple or list containing the access key
                     and secret key, in that order.
                     If this value is None, the credentials in the boto
                     config will be used.
    """
```

```
    if not accounts:
        creds = (boto.config.get('Credentials', 'aws_access_key_id'),
                boto.config.get('Credentials', 'aws_secret_access_key'))
        accounts = {'main' : creds}
    running_instances = {}
    for account_name in accounts:
        running_instances[account_name] = {}
        ak, sk = accounts[account_name]
        for region in boto.ec2.regions():
            conn = region.connect(aws_access_key_id=ak,
                                  aws_secret_access_key=sk)
            filters={'instance-state-name' : 'running'}
            instances = []
            reservations = conn.get_all_instances(filters=filters)
            for r in reservations:
                instances += r.instances
            if instances:
                running_instances[account_name][region.name] = instances
    if not quiet:
        print_running_instances(running_instances)
    return running_instances

if __name__ == '__main__':
    find_all_running_instances()
```

Here's an example of the script in use and the output produced:

```
>>> from ec2_find_all_running_instances import *
>>> find_all_running_instances()
The following running instances were found
    Account: main
        Region: us-east-1
            An t1.micro instance: i-9221f9fd
                Tags={u'midoc': ''}
            An t1.micro instance: i-b62057d6
                Tags={u'paws': ''}
{'main': {u'us-east-1': [Instance:i-9221f9fd, Instance:i-b62057d6]}}
```

2.12 Monitoring the Performance of Your Instance

Problem

Now that your instance is up and running, you want to monitor its performance and load.

Solution

Use CloudWatch to get detailed data about your instance.

Discussion

Monitoring the health and performance of your instances is an important part of operating any website or service. The CloudWatch service provides the ability to get detailed monitoring data about your EC2 instances and other AWS resources.

Example 2-13 illustrates how to enable monitoring on an EC2 instance and then retrieve various types of monitoring data for that instance.

First, we will find our existing instance and enable CloudWatch monitoring. A free tier of CloudWatch monitoring includes a limited set of metrics measured on a five-minute interval. There is an additional hourly charge for monitoring your instance if you want access to more metrics or finer-grained measurements. See *http://aws.amazon.com/cloudwatch/* for details.

Example 2-13. Enable Monitoring Your Instance

```
>>> import boto
>>> ec2 = boto.connect_ec2()
>>> reservations = ec2.get_all_instances(filters={'paws' : None})
>>> instance = reservations[0].instances[0]  ❶
>>> instance.monitor()
```

❶ Find the instance we want to start monitoring. This example assumes it is the instance we started in an earlier recipe and is tagged with the label paws.

Example 2-14 shows how to query CloudWatch for data about your instance. It can take a few minutes for CloudWatch to actually start collecting data after you enable monitoring, so it's best to wait a bit before trying this part.

Example 2-14. Monitor Your Instance

```
>>> cw = boto.connect_cloudwatch()
>>> metrics = cw.list_metrics()  ❶
>>> my_metrics = []
>>> for metric in metrics:  ❷
...    if 'InstanceId' in metric.dimensions:
...       if instance.id in metric.dimensions['InstanceId']:
...          my_metrics.append(metric)
...
>>> my_metrics
[Metric:CPUUtilization(InstanceId,i-76894c16), Metric:DiskReadOps(InstanceId,i-76894c16),
Metric:NetworkIn(InstanceId,i-76894c16), Metric:DiskWriteOps(InstanceId,i-76894c16),
Metric:DiskWriteBytes(InstanceId,i-76894c16), Metric:DiskReadBytes(InstanceId,i-76894c16),
Metric:NetworkOut(InstanceId,i-76894c16)]
```

```
>>> import boto.utils
>>> start_time = boto.utils.parse_ts(instance.launch_time)  ❸
>>> start_time
datetime.datetime(2011, 9, 6, 15, 3, 47)
>>> import datetime
>>> end_time = datetime.datetime.utcnow()  ❹
>>> end_time
datetime.datetime(2011, 9, 6, 16, 9, 25, 61216)
>>> metric = my_metrics[0]
>>> metric
Metric:CPUUtilization(InstanceId,i-76894c16)
>>> metric.Units  ❺
['Seconds', 'Microseconds', 'Milliseconds', 'Bytes', 'Kilobytes', 'Megabytes',
'Gigabytes', 'Terabytes', 'Bits', 'Kilobits', 'Megabits', 'Gigabits', 'Terabits',
'Percent', 'Count', 'Bytes/Second', 'Kilobytes/Second', 'Megabytes/Second',
'Gigabytes/Second', 'Terabytes/Second', 'Bits/Second', 'Kilobits/Second',
'Megabits/Second', 'Gigabits/Second', 'Terabits/Second', 'Count/Second', None]
>>> metric.Statistics  ❻
['Minimum', 'Maximum', 'Sum', 'Average', 'SampleCount']
>>> cpu_samples = metric.query(start_time, end_time, 'Average')  ❼
>>> cpu_samples[0]
{u'Timestamp': datetime.datetime(2011, 9, 6, 15, 3), u'Average': 0.38999999999999996,
u'Unit': u'Percent'}
>>> len(cpu_samples)
61
>>> my_metrics
[Metric:CPUUtilization(InstanceId,i-76894c16), Metric:DiskReadOps(InstanceId,i-76894c16),
Metric:NetworkIn(InstanceId,i-76894c16), Metric:DiskWriteOps(InstanceId,i-76894c16),
Metric:DiskWriteBytes(InstanceId,i-76894c16), Metric:DiskReadBytes(InstanceId,i-76894c16),
Metric:NetworkOut(InstanceId,i-76894c16)]
>>> disk_read_metric = my_metrics[-2]
>>> disk_read_metric
Metric:DiskReadBytes(InstanceId,i-76894c16)
>>> disk_samples = disk_read_metric.query(start_time, end_time, 'Maximum', 'Bytes')  ❽
>>> len(disk_samples)
61
>>> disk_samples[0]
{u'Timestamp': datetime.datetime(2011, 9, 6, 15, 13), u'Average': 0.0, u'Unit': u'Bytes'}
>>> network_out_metric = my_metrics[-1]
>>> metric
Metric:NetworkOut(InstanceId,i-76894c16)
>>> net_samples = metric.query(start_time, end_time, 'Maximum', period=120)  ❾
>>> len(net_samples)
31
>>> net_samples[0]
```

```
{u'Timestamp': datetime.datetime(2011, 9, 7, 7, 28), u'Maximum': 28.0, u'Unit': u'Bytes'}
>>>
```

❶ This will return a list of all of the available CloudWatch metrics. Each will be represented by a `Metric` object. The contents of this list will vary for each user, depending on the number of instances you have running and the number of other monitorable resources (SQS queues, SNS topics, etc.) that the account has created.

❷ This code will loop through all available metrics and create a list, called `my_met rics`, consisting of only the metrics that are relevant to this particular EC2 instance.

❸ In order to query CloudWatch for data, we need to specify the timeframe that we are interested in by providing a `start_time` and an `end_time`. For this example, we are going to use the launch time of the instance as our start time and the current time as our end time. The `Instance` object has a `launch_time` attribute, but it is a string representation of the timestamp, and we need a Python `datetime` object. We can use the `boto` utility function `parse_ts` to convert the string to a `datetime` object.

❹ The `utcnow` function will return a `datetime` object representing the current time in UTC.

❺ Data returned by CloudWatch always has an associated `Unit` that represents the unit of measure. The `Units` attribute of the Metric class is a list of all available units. For example, if you are asking for data about network output, you could choose between `Bytes/Second`, `Kilobytes/Second`, `Megabytes/Second`, etc.

❻ You can also choose different `Statistics` when you query CloudWatch for data. `Statistics` defines how the data is aggregated over time. You may want, for example, the `Average` value or the `Minimum` or `Maximum`.

 For more information about Units and Statistics in CloudWatch, check out *http://docs.amazonwebservices.com/AmazonCloudWatch/ latest/DeveloperGuide/cloudwatch_concepts.html*.

❼ First, we will select the metric for CPU Utilization. We locate the `Metric` object in our list of metrics and then use the `query` method of the object to issue the query to CloudWatch. This returns a list of Python dictionary objects representing the samples from CloudWatch. Each sample consists of a timestamp, a unit of measurement, and the actual sample value.

❽ Here, we query the `DiskReadBytes` metric. Rather than the average, we are asking for the maximum value observed within the period.

❾ Finally, we query the `NetworkOut` metric, asking for the maximum value within each sample period. In addition, rather than relying on the default granularity of 60 seconds (the minimum), we will instead specify a period of 120 seconds. The period value must be a multiple of 60.

2.13 Getting Notifications

Problem

You have monitoring enabled on your EC2 instance. Now you would like to get notified when certain conditions arise.

Solution

Use CloudWatch Alarms to set up notification.

Discussion

All of the recipes in this book are focused on the EC2 and S3 services. However, for this particular recipe we will dip our toe into one other Amazon Web Service, the Simple Notification Service (*http://aws.amazon.com/sns*). This service provides a very simple yet robust publish and subscribe (*http://en.wikipedia.org/wiki/Publish/subscribe*) service, which does a great job as a scalable method of implementing communication between processes or services. We won't be able to cover the details of SNS in detail, but this example will show you how to leverage SNS to quickly enable email notification of CloudWatch events using alarms (*http://docs.amazonwebservices.com/Amazon CloudWatch/latest/DeveloperGuide/cloudwatch_concepts.html#CloudWatchAlarms*).

The following commands assume that you have signed up for SNS with your AWS account. The first step in enabling CloudWatch alarms is to create an SNS topic to which events can be published. People or systems that are interested in these events can then subscribe to the topic. When you subscribe, you can select a number of different notification protocols. For example, you could select http, which would cause a JSON payload containing the message contents to be POSTed via HTTP to the endpoint you provide. Or you can subscribe via SQS (Simple Queue Service), which will place a message in an SQS queue. For this example, we will use the email protocol to send an email message to the specified email address each time an alarm is fired.

Example 2-15. Configuring SNS for CloudWatch Alarms

```
>>> import boto
>>> sns = boto.connect_sns()
>>> sns.create_topic('paws_cloudwatch')
{u'CreateTopicResponse': {u'ResponseMetadata': {u'RequestId': u'73721b87-
da0e-11e0-99a4-59769425d805'},
 u'CreateTopicResult': {u'TopicArn': u'arn:aws:sns:us-
east-1:084307701560:paws_cloudwatch'}}}
>>> topic_arn = _['CreateTopicResponse']['CreateTopicResult']['TopicArn']
>>> topic_arn
u'arn:aws:sns:us-east-1:084307701560:paws_cloudwatch'
>>> sns.subscribe(topic_arn, 'email', 'mitch@garnaat.org')
{u'SubscribeResponse': {u'SubscribeResult': {u'SubscriptionArn': u'pending confirmation'},
 u'ResponseMetadata': {u'RequestId': u'd4a846fd-da0e-11e0-bcf1-37db33647dea'}}}
>>>
```

Make note of the `topic_arn`, as that identifier will be needed later, when we create the Alarm object.

Shortly after typing the commands above, you should receive an email message from AWS at the address subscribed. This email will contain a link that you need to click on to complete the subscription process. If you click on it, you should see a page like Figure 2-1 in your browser.

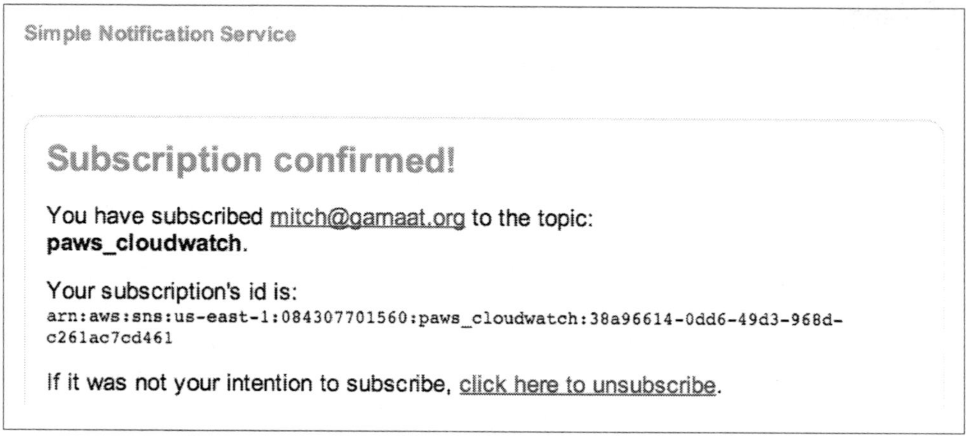

Simple Notification Service

Subscription confirmed!

You have subscribed mitch@garnaat.org to the topic: **paws_cloudwatch**.

Your subscription's id is:
arn:aws:sns:us-east-1:084307701560:paws_cloudwatch:38a96614-0dd6-49d3-968d-c261ac7cd461

If it was not your intention to subscribe, click here to unsubscribe.

Figure 2-1. SNS Confirmation Page

With that complete, we have successfully established the SNS topic that can be used for publishing CloudWatch alarms, and we have also subscribed to that topic so we will receive an email message each time an alarm is published to the topic. The next step is to configure the alarm in CloudWatch.

Example 2-16. Creating a CloudWatch Alarm

```
>>> import boto
>>> cw = boto.connect_cloudwatch()
>>> my_metrics = cw.list_metrics(dimensions={'InstanceId':'i-76894c16'})
>>> my_metrics
[Metric:DiskReadOps, Metric:NetworkOut, Metric:NetworkIn, Metric:DiskReadBytes,
Metric:CPUUtilization, Metric:DiskWriteBytes, Metric:DiskWriteOps]
>>> metric = my_metrics[4]
>>> metric
Metric:CPUUtilization
>>> alarm = metric.create_alarm(name='CPUAlarm', comparison='>', threshold=80.0, period=60,
evaluation_periods=2, statistic='Average',
alarm_actions=['arn:aws:sns:us-east-1:084307701560:paws_cloudwatch'],
ok_actions=['arn:aws:sns:us-east-1:084307701560:paws_cloudwatch'])
>>> alarm
MetricAlarm:CPUAlarm[CPUUtilization(Average) GreaterThanThreshold 80.0]
>>> alarm.set_state('ALARM', 'Testing my alarm', '100')
True
>>> alarm.describe_history()
[AlarmHistory:CPUAlarm[Successfully executed action arn:aws:sns:us-
```

```
east-1:084307701560:paws_cloudwatch at 2011-09-20 14:32:14.355000],
AlarmHistory:CPUAlarm[Alarm updated from ALARM to OK at 2011-09-20 14:32:14.354000],
AlarmHistory:CPUAlarm[Successfully executed action arn:aws:sns:us-
east-1:084307701560:paws_cloudwatch at 2011-09-20 14:32:13.562000],
AlarmHistory:CPUAlarm[Alarm updated from OK to ALARM at 2011-09-20 14:32:13.561000],
AlarmHistory:CPUAlarm[Successfully executed action arn:aws:sns:us-
east-1:084307701560:paws_cloudwatch at 2011-09-20 14:27:31.440000],
AlarmHistory:CPUAlarm[Alarm updated from INSUFFICIENT_DATA to OK at 2011-09-20
14:27:31.439000],
AlarmHistory:CPUAlarm[Alarm "CPUAlarm" created at 2011-09-20 14:27:30.815000]]
>>>
```

In the example above, after creating my alarm and associating it with my metric in
CloudWatch, I then simulated a change in state with the call to set_alarm_state. This
call gives you a handy way to test out your alarm and your notification mechanism so
you have confidence that when a real alarm state is encountered, you will know about
it. If everything is working properly, you should receive an email that looks something
like this at the account that was subscribed to the SNS topic:

```
From: AWS Notifications <no-reply@sns.amazonaws.com>
Date: September 20, 2011 10:32:13 AM EDT
To: "mitch@garnaat.org" <mitch@garnaat.org>
Subject: [ALARM] Alarm "CPUAlarm" in US - N. Virginia is now in state ALARM

You are receiving this email because your Amazon CloudWatch Alarm "CPUAlarm" in the US
- N. Virginia region has entered the ALARM state, because "Testing my alarm" at
"Tuesday 20 September, 2011 14:32:13 UTC".

View this alarm in the AWS Management Console:
https://console.aws.amazon.com/cloudwatch/home?region=us-
east-1#s=Alarms&alarm=CPUAlarm

Alarm Details:
- Name:                      CPUAlarm
- Description:               High Average CPU Usage Alarm
- State Change:              OK -> ALARM
- Reason for State Change:   Testing my alarm
- Timestamp:                 Tuesday 20 September, 2011 14:32:13 UTC

Threshold:
- The alarm is in the ALARM state when the metric is GreaterThanThreshold 75.0 for 60
seconds.

Monitored Metric:
- MetricNamespace:           AWS/EC2
- MetricName:                CPUUtilization
- Dimensions:                [InstanceId = i-0ef5756e]
- Period:                    60 seconds
- Statistic:                 Average
- Unit:                      Percent
```

```
State Change Actions:
- OK: [arn:aws:sns:us-east-1:084307701560:paws_cloudwatch]
- ALARM: [arn:aws:sns:us-east-1:084307701560:paws_cloudwatch]
- INSUFFICIENT_DATA: [arn:aws:sns:us-east-1:084307701560:paws_cloudwatch]

--
```

There. That was easy, wasn't it? Okay, it wasn't really all that easy. There are a lot of steps and many opportunities to goof things up, but at least that gives you the nuts and bolts of how to get this very sophisticated plumbing installed in your environment. There will be times when you need to work at that nuts and bolts level, but to help people get started with alarms, here's a high-level Python function that makes it much easier to get basic email notifications working.

Example 2-17. Easy Email Notifications

```
import os
import boto

def easy_alarm(instance_id,
               alarm_name,
               email_addresses,
               metric_name,
               comparison,
               threshold,
               period,
               eval_periods,
               statistics):
    """
    Create a CloudWatch alarm for a given instance.  You can choose
    the metric and dimension you want to associate with the alarm
    and you can provide a list of email addresses that will be
    notified when the alarm fires.

    instance_id      The unique identifier of the instance you wish to
                     monitoring.

    alarm_name       A short but meaningful name for your alarm.

    email_addresses  A list of email addresses that you want to
                     have notified when the alarm fires.

    metric_name      The name of the Metric you want to be notified
                     about.  Valid values are:
                     DiskReadBytes|DiskWriteBytes|
                     DiskReadOps|DiskWriteOps|
                     NetworkIn|NetworkOut|
                     CPUUtilization

    comparison       The comparison operator.  Valid values are:
                     >= | > | < | <=

    threshold        The threshold value that the metric will
                     be compared against.
```

```
period          The granularity of the returned data.
                Minimum value is 60 (seconds) and valid values
                must be multiples of 60.

eval_periods    The number of periods over which the alarm
                must be measured before triggering notification.

statistics      The statistic to apply.  Valid values are:
                SampleCount | Average | Sum | Minimum | Maximum

"""
# Create a connection to the required services
ec2 = boto.connect_ec2()
sns = boto.connect_sns()
cw = boto.connect_cloudwatch()

# Make sure the instance in question exists and
# is being monitored with CloudWatch.
rs = ec2.get_all_instances(filters={'instance-id', instance_id})
if len(rs) != 1:
    raise ValueError('Unable to find instance: %s' % instance_id)

instance = rs[0].instances[0]
instance.monitor()

# Create the SNS Topic
topic_name = 'CWAlarm-%s' % alarm_name
print 'Creating SNS topic: %s' % topic_name
response = sns.create_topic(topic_name)
topic_arn = response['CreateTopicResponse']['CreateTopicResult']['TopicArn']
print 'Topic ARN: %s' % topic_arn

# Subscribe the email addresses to SNS Topic
for addr in email_addresses:
    print 'Subscribing %s to Topic %s' % (addr, topic_arn)
    sns.subscribe(topic_arn, 'email', addr)

# Now find the Metric we want to be notified about
metric = cw.list_metrics(dimensions={'InstanceId':instance_id},
                         metric_name=metric_name)[0]
print 'Found: %s' % metric

# Now create Alarm for the metric
print 'Creating alarm'
alarm = metric.create_alarm(name=alarm_name, comparison=comparison,
                            threshold=threshold, period=period,
                            evaluationn_periods=eval_periods,
                            statistics=statistics,
                            alarm_actions=[topic_arn],
                            ok_actions=[topic_arn])
```

2.14 Storing Custom Data in CloudWatch

Problem

You have your own custom metrics that you would like to be able to monitor.

Solution

Use CloudWatch Custom Metrics to publish your data to CloudWatch.

Discussion

CloudWatch provides a wide-range of standard metrics that can be monitored or incorporated into alarms. However, many applications have custom data that is important to monitor, such as query times from a database or total disk usage on some partition.

The PutMetricData request of CloudWatch allows you to define your own metrics and store your own data in CloudWatch and then use the existing tools and GUIs to access and graph that data.

In this example, we will write a simple script that simply stores 100 integer values in a custom metric over a period of time. We will then use the same query mechanism we used previously on standard CloudWatch metrics to retrieve the data from Cloud-Watch.

Note that if the data being gathered and stored in CloudWatch comes from an EC2 instance, that means that requests to CloudWatch will have to happen on that instance. That, in turn, means that you will have to have some EC2 credentials available on the instance. It is dangerous, however, to store the main credentials for your account on any server that is accessible from the outside world, so be very careful and think through how you want to handle this. Specifically, you might want to check out Recipe 2.15 for suggestions about passing safer credentials to instances.

Example 2-18. CloudWatch Custom Metrics

```
>>> import boto, time, datetime
>>> start_time = datetime.datetime.utcnow()
>>> cw = boto.connect_cloudwatch()
>>> for i in range(0,100):
...    cw.put_metric_data('PAWS', 'FooCount', i)
...    time.sleep(5)
...
True
True
True
True
...
>>> end_time = datetime.datetime.utcnow()
>>> cw.list_metrics(namespace='PAWS')
```

```
[Metric:FooCount]
>>> metric.query(start_time, end_time, 'Maximum')
[{u'Timestamp': datetime.datetime(2011, 9, 20, 21, 30),
u'Maximum': 78.0, u'Unit': u'None'},
{u'Timestamp': datetime.datetime(2011, 9, 20, 21, 27),
u'Maximum': 42.0, u'Unit': u'None'},
{u'Timestamp': datetime.datetime(2011, 9, 20, 21, 24),
u'Maximum': 7.0, u'Unit': u'None'},
{u'Timestamp': datetime.datetime(2011, 9, 20, 21, 28),
u'Maximum': 54.0, u'Unit': u'None'},
{u'Timestamp': datetime.datetime(2011, 9, 20, 21, 29),
u'Maximum': 66.0, u'Unit': u'None'},
{u'Timestamp': datetime.datetime(2011, 9, 20, 21, 25),
u'Maximum': 18.0, u'Unit': u'None'},
{u'Timestamp': datetime.datetime(2011, 9, 20, 21, 32),
u'Maximum': 99.0, u'Unit': u'None'},
{u'Timestamp': datetime.datetime(2011, 9, 20, 21, 22),
u'Maximum': 1.0, u'Unit': u'None'},
{u'Timestamp': datetime.datetime(2011, 9, 20, 21, 31),
u'Maximum': 90.0, u'Unit': u'None'},
{u'Timestamp': datetime.datetime(2011, 9, 20, 21, 26),
u'Maximum': 30.0, u'Unit': u'None'}]
>>> metric.query(start_time, end_time, 'Average')
[{u'Timestamp': datetime.datetime(2011, 9, 20, 21, 30),
u'Average': 72.5, u'Unit': u'None'},
{u'Timestamp': datetime.datetime(2011, 9, 20, 21, 27),
u'Average': 36.5, u'Unit': u'None'},
{u'Timestamp': datetime.datetime(2011, 9, 20, 21, 24),
u'Average': 3.5, u'Unit': u'None'},
{u'Timestamp': datetime.datetime(2011, 9, 20, 21, 28),
u'Average': 48.5, u'Unit': u'None'},
{u'Timestamp': datetime.datetime(2011, 9, 20, 21, 29),
u'Average': 60.5, u'Unit': u'None'},
{u'Timestamp': datetime.datetime(2011, 9, 20, 21, 25),
u'Average': 13.0, u'Unit': u'None'},
{u'Timestamp': datetime.datetime(2011, 9, 20, 21, 32),
u'Average': 95.0, u'Unit': u'None'},
{u'Timestamp': datetime.datetime(2011, 9, 20, 21, 22),
u'Average': 1.0, u'Unit': u'None'},
{u'Timestamp': datetime.datetime(2011, 9, 20, 21, 31),
u'Average': 84.5, u'Unit': u'None'},
{u'Timestamp': datetime.datetime(2011, 9, 20, 21, 26),
u'Average': 24.5, u'Unit': u'None'}]
>>>
```

2.15 Executing Custom Scripts upon Instance Startup

Problem

You need to run custom scripts each time a new instance is started.

Solution

Use the `user_data` feature to pass scripts and/or data to your newly started instance.

Discussion

Once you get beyond the experimentation phase with EC2, you will quickly find that in addition to just starting an instance, you want to prepare that instance for a particular task. Why would you be starting an instance if you didn't have an important job for it to perform? It turns out there are two main schools of thought regarding how best to accomplish this:

Custom images

> This approach focuses on starting with a plain vanilla image and then configuring all of the required software necessary to perform the desired task. Once everything is installed and configured, you create a new image based on this fully configured image, and that becomes the image that you use. When an instance based on this image is started, it has everything it needs to perform its task.

Startup time configuration

> This approach also starts with a plain vanilla image, but all of the installation and configuration is done when the instance starts up. This could be accomplished with scripts and/or data that are passed the instance at startup time, or it could use a more sophisticated, centralized configuration service like Puppet (*http://puppetlabs .com/*) or Chef (*http://opscode.com/*).

Deciding which is right for you is a trade-off. Custom images provide quick start time and fewer dependencies but are less flexible. Each time you want to update the software on the image, you have to rebundle it. On the other hand, using scripts or configuration engines makes it easy to tweak the configuration at any time and see the effect as soon as you start a new instance. However, depending on how much installation and configuration is required, it could take a considerable amount of time for a new instance to become fully operational, and if you are installing software from public package repositories, there is always a chance that they may be unavailable, which would prevent the script from completing.

Many people end up using some combination of the two approaches. Big packages like databases and web servers can be built into the image, because they take a long time to install and don't change that often, whereas application code and data can be configured through scripts. This is a complicated topic and very application-specific; however, I do want to show a couple of examples of passing data and scripts to newly started instances to give you some idea of the power and flexibility that are available to you.

Our first recipe will use the `user-data scripts` popularized by Eric Hammond (*http:// alestic.com/*). This technique works out of the box with modern Ubuntu images as well as with the Amazon Linux AMI (*http://aws.amazon.com/amazon-linux-ami/*). You can simply pass a shell script as `user-data` when the instance is launched, and the shell

---

script will be executed as root on the instance at launch. The example script, taken from the Ubuntu website, simply writes a message to a file on the file system. After the instance is up and running, you can log in and see if the file exists.

Example 2-19. A Simple User-Data Script

```
>>> from ec2_launch_instance import launch_instance
>>> script = """#!/bin/sh
... echo "Hello World.  The time is now $(date -R)!" | tee /root/output.txt
... """
>>> instance, cmdshell = launch_instance(user_data=script)
Security Group: paws already authorized
waiting for instance
.
.
.
.
done
SSH Connection refused, will retry in 5 seconds
>>> cmdshell.shell()

       _|  _|_  )
      _|  (   -  /    Amazon Linux AMI
      __|\__|__|

See /usr/share/doc/system-release/ for latest release notes.
No packages needed for security; 1 packages available
[ec2-user@domU-12-31-39-00-E4-53 ~]# sudo su
[ec2-user@domU-12-31-39-00-E4-53 ~]# cd /root
[ec2-user@domU-12-31-39-00-E4-53 ~]# ls
output.txt
[ec2-user@domU-12-31-39-00-E4-53 ~]# cat output.txt
Hello World.  The time is now Wed, 21 Sep 2011 23:53:51 +0000!
[ec2-user@domU-12-31-39-00-E4-53 ~]# exit
[ec2-user@domU-12-31-39-00-E4-53 ~]$ logout

*** EOF
>>> instance.terminate()
>>>
```

As you can see, we pass the shell script in as user_data when we launch the instance, and when we log in after launch, we can see that the file *output.txt* has, in fact, been created, indicating that the script has been run. The mechanism behind this is quite simple. A special program is run at boot time that inspects the user_data passed to the instance, and if it begins with a *shebang* (#!), it will try to execute the script as code. The script will be run as root, so it has full access to the instance.

The next example will be a bit more ambitious. We will use several key features of a package called CloudInit (*https://help.ubuntu.com/community/CloudInit*), which is sort of a grown-up version of user-data scripts developed by Canonical. The CloudInit package is also automatically supported by modern Ubuntu distros as well as Amazon Linux AMI (*http://aws.amazon.com/amazon-linux-ami/*) images. CloudInit allows you to package up a number of items, such as shell scripts, configuration information, up-start jobs, and the like, in a single MIME multipart package and send the whole package to your instance to be evaluated and executed upon launch. You can even compress the package with `gzip` to pack more stuff into your 16 K limit on `user_data`.

For this example, we will be installing a set of `Metric` objects on our newly launched instance. Each `Metric` object will consist of a chunk of Python code that will be responsible for gathering some data from our running instance and then storing that data as a custom metric in CloudWatch. This custom metric data can then be queried using any existing CloudWatch-enabled tool and can be hooked into alarms in SNS, as shown in Recipe 2.13.

Before we get started with the code, we should first deal with a security question. If each of our `Metric` objects that we install needs to write custom metric data to Cloud-Watch, we will need to have AWS credentials on the instances. This can be dangerous! The `access_key` and `secret_key` associated with your AWS account are the keys to your castle. Anyone who gains access to these can stop all of your instances, delete all of your EBS volumes and snapshots, and wipe out all of your S3 objects. You need to manage those credentials very carefully and, somehow, storing them in clear text on a server that is potentially accessible to the Internet doesn't sound like a good way to manage them.

Fortunately, AWS has a very useful service called IAM (Identity and Access Management) that allows you to create users within your AWS account. These users have their own `access_key` and `secret_key`, separate from your account credentials. You can create and delete these users at will, either through the web console or via the API. In addition, each of these users can have JSON policies associated with them to finely tune which services each user has access to, which requests are allowed for each service, and which resources they can access.

Example 2-20 shows a small Python script that uses `boto` to create a new user and to associate a JSON policy with that user that gives the user access to a single request in a single service, the `PutMetricData` request of CloudWatch. It then creates a *boto.cfg* file that contains those credentials. We will need this file later in the example.

We can then pass these limited credentials to our newly launched instances and be comforted in knowing that, even if someone did break into our server and grab those credentials, the worst he or she could do would be to store bogus data in CloudWatch. Still not a good thing, but a risk that seems manageable.

Example 2-20. Creating a Restricted User with IAM

```
import boto

# Create a restricted user using IAM

# The following JSON policy was generated using the
# AWS Policy Generator app.
# http://awspolicygen.s3.amazonaws.com/policygen.html
```

```
policy_json = """{
  "Statement": [
    {
      "Sid": "Stmt1316576423630",
      "Action": [
        "cloudwatch:PutMetricData"
      ],
      "Effect": "Allow",
      "Resource": "*"
    }
  ]
}"""

def create_restricted_user(user_name):
    """
    Create a new user in this account.  The user will be
    restricted by the JSON policy document above.
    This function returns a tuple containing the access key
    and secret key for the new account.

    user_name The name of the new user.
    """
    iam = boto.connect_iam()
    user = iam.create_user(user_name)
    keys = iam.create_access_key(user_name)
    response = iam.put_user_policy(user_name,
                                  'CloudWatchPutMetricData',
                                  policy_json)
    fp = open('boto.cfg', 'w')
    fp.write('[Credentials]\n')
    fp.write('aws_access_key_id = %s\n' % keys.access_key_id)
    fp.write('aws_secret_access_key = %s\n' % keys.secret_access_key)
    fp.close()
```

With that detail out of the way, we can focus on defining our custom metric code and
getting it installed and running on newly launched instances. The metric we will use
for this example is disk usage (what percentage of space on our root volume is available). This is not data that you can get from standard CloudWatch metrics, and it is
useful to know, since it's rarely a good thing when your server runs out of disk space.
Below, you will see the Python code that will calculate available disk space (as a percentage of total space) and store that as a custom metric in CloudWatch.

Example 2-21. Custom Metric for Disk Usage

```
#!/usr/bin/env python
import boto
import time
import datetime
import os

def main():
    cw = boto.connect_cloudwatch()
    md = boto.utils.get_instance_metadata()
```

```
    now = datetime.datetime.utcnow()
    stats = os.statvfs('/')
    total = float(stats.f_blocks * stats.f_bsize)
    available = float(stats.f_bavail * stats.f_bsize)
    percent_used = int(100 - 100 * (available / total))
    print 'metric_disk_usage: %d' % percent_used
    cw.put_metric_data(namespace='PAWS',
                       name='DiskUsage',
                       value=percent_used,
                       timestamp=now,
                       unit='Percent',
                       dimensions=[{'InstanceId' : md['instance-id']}])

if __name__ == "__main__":
    main()
```

Now that we have our metric code, we need to get it installed and running on our newly launched instances. Example 2-22 is responsible for constructing the CloudInit-compatible user data that will be passed to the instance. This code assumes that you have stored the *boto.cfg* file generated above along with metric code together in the same directory. It will package those items, along with a couple of other things, into a single MIME multipart file. But how will CloudInit know what to do with our config file and metric code? Well, that's where the part_handler comes in, the final piece of the puzzle. The part_handler can tell CloudInit about new types of files that it is able to handle, and then whenever CloudInit comes across that type of file, it will call our part_handler to take care of it. Example 2-22 shows the part_handler.

Example 2-22. Custom CloudInit Part Handler

```
#part-handler

import os

def list_types():
    """
    Return a list of mime-types that are handled by this module.
    """
    return(['text/x-config', 'text/x-metric'])

def handle_part(data, ctype, filename, payload):
    """
    data:     the cloudinit object
    ctype:    '__begin__', '__end__', or the specific mime-type of the part
    filename: the filename for the part, or dynamically generated part if
              no filename is given attribute is present
    payload:  the content of the part (empty for begin or end)
    """
    if ctype == 'text/x-config':
        path = os.path.join('/etc', filename)
        fp = open(path, 'w')
        fp.write(payload)
        fp.close()
        print '==== wrote %s payload to %s ====' % (ctype, path)
```

```
elif ctype == 'text/x-metric':
    # Save metric command as an executable
    path = os.path.join('/usr/local/sbin', filename)
    fp = open(path, 'w')
    fp.write(payload)
    fp.close()
    os.chmod(path, 0755)
    # Add an entry to tell cron to run this every minute
    path = os.path.join('/etc/cron.d', filename)
    fp = open(path, 'w')
    fp.write('root /usr/local/sbin/%s' % filename)
    fp.close()
```

The final piece of the puzzle is the code that bundles everything up to send to the instance when we run it. Let's take a look at Example 2-23.

Example 2-23. Custom CloudInit Packager

```
from email.mime.multipart import MIMEMultipart
from email.mime.text import MIMEText
import gzip
import cStringIO
import os

script = """#!/bin/sh
echo "Installing boto..."
cd /root
git clone git://github.com/boto/boto.git
cd boto
python setup.py install
echo "...done"
"""

cloud_config = """
packages:
 - python-setuptools

runcmd:
 - [ easy_install, boto ]
"""

def create_txt_part(path, subtype, filename=None):
    fp = open(path)
    s = fp.read()
    fp.close()
    txt = MIMEText(s, _subtype=subtype)
    if filename:
        txt.add_header('Content-Disposition',
                       'attachment', filename=filename)
    return txt

def build_userdata(metric_dir):
    mp = MIMEMultipart()
    # Add our part handler
    path = os.path.join(metric_dir, 'metric_part_handler.py')
```

```
txt = create_txt_part(path, 'part-handler', 'metric_part_handler.py')
mp.attach(txt)
# Add the boto config file
path = os.path.join(metric_dir, 'boto.cfg')
txt = create_txt_part(path, 'x-config', 'boto.cfg')
mp.attach(txt)
# Add the cloud-config
txt = MIMEText(cloud_config, _subtype='cloud-config')
mp.attach(txt)
# Add disk metric
path = os.path.join(metric_dir, 'metric_disk_usage')
txt = create_txt_part(path, 'x-metric', 'metric_disk_usage')
mp.attach(txt)

gfileobj = cStringIO.StringIO()
gfile = gzip.GzipFile(fileobj=gfileobj, mode='wb')
gfile.write(mp.as_string())
gfile.close()

return gfileobj.getvalue()
```

Example 2-24 shows the interactive session where we build our user_data and launch our instance.

Example 2-24. A Simple User-Data Script

```
>>> from ec2_custom_script_server import build_userdata
>>> from ec2_launch_instance import launch_instance
>>> user_data = build_userdata(metric_dir='./metrics')
>>> instance, cmd = launch_instance(user_data=user_data)
```

And finally, after the instance has been running for a bit, Example 2-25 shows the interactive session where we query CloudWatch for our new custom metric data.

Example 2-25. A Simple User-Data Script

```
>>> import boto
>>> cw = boto.connect_cloudwatch()
>>> ec2 = boto.connect_ec2()
>>> import datetime
>>> metrics = cw.list_metrics(namespace='PAWS', metric_name='DiskUsage')
>>> metrics
[Metric:DiskUsage]
>>> metric = metrics[0]
>>> r = ec2.get_all_instances([metric.dimensions['InstanceId'][0]])
>>> instance = r[0].instances[0]
>>> start_time = boto.utils.parse_ts(instance.launch_time)
>>> end_time = datetime.datetime.utcnow()
>>> metric.query(start_time, end_time, ['Maximum'])
[{u'Maximum': 12.0,
  u'Timestamp': datetime.datetime(2011, 9, 22, 15, 32),
  u'Unit': u'Percent'},
 {u'Maximum': 12.0,
  u'Timestamp': datetime.datetime(2011, 9, 22, 15, 17),
  u'Unit': u'Percent'},
```

```
{u'Maximum': 12.0,
 u'Timestamp': datetime.datetime(2011, 9, 22, 15, 31),
 u'Unit': u'Percent'},
{u'Maximum': 12.0,
 u'Timestamp': datetime.datetime(2011, 9, 22, 14, 44),
 u'Unit': u'Percent'},
...
{u'Maximum': 12.0,
 u'Timestamp': datetime.datetime(2011, 9, 22, 14, 39),
 u'Unit': u'Percent'}]
```

## CHAPTER 3

S3 Recipes

3.1 Create a Bucket

Problem

Before you can store anything in S3, you need to first create a bucket to contain the objects.

Solution

Use the `create_bucket` method to create a new bucket.

Discussion

Example 3-1 shows a function that takes the name of the bucket you want to create as a parameter. It will then try to create that bucket. If the bucket already exists, it will print an error.

Example 3-1. Create a Bucket

```
import boto

def create_bucket(bucket_name):
    """
    Create a bucket.  If the bucket already exists and you have
    access to it, no error will be returned by AWS.
    Note that bucket names are global to S3
    so you need to choose a unique name.
    """
    s3 = boto.connect_s3()

    # First let's see if we already have a bucket of this name.
    # The lookup method will return a Bucket object if the
    # bucket exists and we have access to it or None.
    bucket = s3.lookup(bucket_name)
    if bucket:
        print 'Bucket (%s) already exists' % bucket_name
```

```
    else:
        # Let's try to create the bucket.  This will fail if
        # the bucket has already been created by someone else.
        try:
            bucket = s3.create_bucket(bucket_name)
        except s3.provider.storage_create_error, e:
            print 'Bucket (%s) is owned by another user' % bucket_name
return bucket
```

3.2 Create a Bucket in a Specific Location

Problem

You want to create a bucket in a specific geographic location.

Solution

Use the location parameter to the create_bucket method to specify the location of the new bucket.

Discussion

Originally, there was just a single S3 endpoint and all data was stored in one region or location, the eastern United States. Over time, however, the S3 service has expanded, and there are now five region-specific endpoints:

- US Standard
- US-West (Northern California)
- EU (Ireland)
- Asia Pacific (Singapore)
- Asia Pacific (Japan)

There is a big difference, however, in the way S3 handles resources and regions. For services like EC2, SimpleDB, SQS, and the like, the regions are treated as completely separate services, and resources cannot be easily shared across these regions. For example, if you want to create an EC2 instance in the EU region, you have to connect to the EC2 EU endpoint to do so, and that instance is unknown to the other EC2 regions. With S3, you specify a Location for the bucket when it is created, but once it is created, you can access the bucket from any of the S3 endpoints. In addition, you can create an EU bucket when you are talking to the US endpoint and vice versa. So, the resource namespace is global to the entire S3 service, across all regions. The main reason you might decide to talk to a region-specific endpoint is to get better latency in your connections.

Example 3-2. Create a Bucket in a Specific Location

```
import boto
from boto.s3.connection import Location

def create_bucket(bucket_name, location=Location.DEFAULT):
    """
    Create a bucket.  If the bucket already exists and you have
    access to it, no error will be returned by AWS.
    Note that bucket names are global to a S3 region or location
    so you need to choose a unique name.

    bucket_name - The name of the bucket to be created.

    location - The location in which the bucket should be
               created.  The Location class is a simple
               enum-like static class that has the following attributes:

               DEFAULT|EU|USWest|APNortheast|APSoutheast
    """
    s3 = boto.connect_s3()

    # First let's see if we already have a bucket of this name.
    # The lookup method will return a Bucket object if the
    # bucket exists and we have access to it or None.
    bucket = s3.lookup(bucket_name)
    if bucket:
        print 'Bucket (%s) already exists' % bucket_name
    else:
        # Let's try to create the bucket.  This will fail if
        # the bucket has already been created by someone else.
        try:
            bucket = s3.create_bucket(bucket_name, location=location)
        except s3.provider.storage_create_error, e:
            print 'Bucket (%s) is owned by another user' % bucket_name
    return bucket
```

3.3 Store Private Data

Problem

You want to store information that can only be accessed with your credentials.

Solution

Use one of the set_contents_from_* methods of the Key object to store the data in an existing S3 bucket.

Discussion

By default, objects stored in S3 are accessible only with the credentials with which they were created. So, just by storing the information in an S3 bucket in the default manner we will keep the data private to the owner.

Example 3-3. Store Private Data

```
import boto

def store_private_data(bucket_name, key_name, path_to_file):
    """
    Write the contents of a local file to S3 and also store custom
    metadata with the object.

    bucket_name   The name of the S3 Bucket.
    key_name      The name of the object containing the data in S3.
    path_to_file  Fully qualified path to local file.
    """
    s3 = boto.connect_s3()
    bucket = s3.lookup(bucket_name)

    # Get a new, blank Key object from the bucket.  This Key object only
    # exists locally until we actually store data in it.
    key = bucket.new_key(key_name)

    # First let's demonstrate how to write string data to the Key
    data = 'This is the content of my key'
    key.set_contents_from_string(data)

    # Now fetch the data from S3 and compare
    stored_key = bucket.lookup(key_name)
    stored_data = stored_key.get_contents_as_string()
    assert stored_data == data

    # Now, overwrite the data with the contents of the file
    key.set_contents_from_filename(path_to_file)

    return key
```

3.4 Store Metadata with an Object

Problem

You want to store additional metadata with an object in S3.

Solution

Use the `x-amz-meta` header to send additional metadata to store with the object in S3.

Discussion

In addition to the data stored in S3 as an object, you can store additional metadata with that object at the time the object is created in S3. This is accomplished by sending additional HTTP headers with the request. The headers are of the form:

```
x-amz-meta-foo: bar
```

This would store the key/value pair foo=bar in the metadata of the object. Fortunately, boto handles all of these details for you, so you simply need to provide a Python dictionary of key/value pairs, as shown in Example 3-4.

Example 3-4. Store Metadata with an Object

```python
import boto

def store_metadata_with_key(bucket_name,
                            key_name,
                            path_to_file,
                            metadata):
    """
    Write the contents of a local file to S3 and also store custom
    metadata with the object.

    bucket_name     The name of the S3 Bucket.
    key_name        The name of the object containing the data in S3.
    path_to_file    Fully qualified path to local file.
    metadata        A Python dict object containing key/value
                    data you would like associated with the object.
                    For example: {'key1':'value1', 'key2':'value2'}
    """
    s3 = boto.connect_s3()
    bucket = s3.lookup(bucket_name)

    # Get a new, blank Key object from the bucket.  This Key object only
    # exists locally until we actually store data in it.
    key = bucket.new_key(key_name)

    # Add the metadata to the Key object
    key.metadata.update(metadata)

    # Now, write the data and metadata to S3
    key.set_contents_from_filename(path_to_file)

    return key

def print_key_metadata(bucket_name, key_name):
    """
    Print the metadata associated with an S3 Key object.

    bucket_name     The name of the S3 Bucket.
    key_name        The name of the object containing the data in S3.
    """
    s3 = boto.connect_s3()
    bucket = s3.lookup(bucket_name)
```

```
key = bucket.lookup(key_name)
print key.metadata
```

3.5 Computing Total Storage Used by a Bucket

Problem

You want to find out how much storage a bucket is using.

Solution

Iterate through all of the keys in the bucket and total the bytes used.

Discussion

Because you are charged for the amount of storage you use in S3, you may want to know how much data is stored in a particular bucket. The only way to do this is to iterate over all of the keys in the bucket and total up the bytes used by each key.

 boto makes this pretty easy, but note that if you have millions of keys in a bucket, it can take a while to iterate over all of them.

Example 3-5. Computing Total Storage Used by a Bucket

```
import boto

def bucket_du(bucket_name):
    """
    Compute the total bytes used by a bucket.
    NOTE: This iterates over every key in the bucket.  If you have millions of
          keys this could take a while.
    """
    s3 = boto.connect_s3()

    total_bytes = 0
    bucket = s3.lookup(bucket_name)
    if bucket:
        for key in bucket:
            total_bytes += key.size
    else:
        print 'Warning: bucket %s was not found!' % bucket_name
    return total_bytes
```

3.6 Copy an Existing Object to Another Bucket

Problem

You have a large object stored in S3 and you want to copy it or move it to another bucket.

Solution

Use the COPY directive to do a server-side copy of the object.

Discussion

The COPY operation was first added to S3 (in beta form) in May 2008. Prior to that, if you wanted to copy or move an object stored in S3, the only option was to download the object from S3 to a client machine and then re-upload the object to the desired location in S3—an expensive and time-consuming operation for large objects.

Fortunately, the COPY operation now allows us to do the hard work on the server-side. The COPY operation requires you to have read permission on the existing object and write permission to the destination bucket. If you want to move the object, you must perform an explicit DELETE operation after COPYing.

Example 3-6. Copy an Existing Object to Another Bucket

```
import boto

def copy_object(src_bucket_name,
                src_key_name,
                dst_bucket_name,
                dst_key_name,
                preserve_metadata=True):
    """
    Copy an existing object to another location.

    src_bucket_name    Bucket containing the existing object.
    src_key_name       Name of the existing object.
    dst_bucket_name    Bucket to which the object is being copied.
    dst_key_name       The name of the new object.
    preserve_metadata  If True, all metadata on the original object
                       will be preserved on the new object.  If False
                       the new object will have the default metadata.
    """
    s3 = boto.connect_s3()
    bucket = s3.lookup(src_bucket_name)

    # Lookup the existing object in S3
    key = bucket.lookup(src_key_name)

    # Copy the key back on to itself, with new metadata
    return key.copy(dst_bucket_name, dst_key_name, preserve_acl=preserve_acl)
```

3.7 Modify the Metadata of an Existing Object

Problem

You want to change the metadata associated with an existing object in S3.

Solution

Use the COPY directive to do an in-place copy of the object with the new metadata.

Discussion

The metadata for an object is defined when the object is created in S3. In the past, if you ever wanted to change the metadata, you had to upload the entire object again. However, the COPY operation now provides a way to change the metadata without incurring the time and cost of uploading the object data.

Example 3-7. Modify the Metadata of an Existing Object

```
import boto

def modify_metadata(bucket_name,
                    key_name,
                    metadata):
    """
    Update the metadata with an existing object.

    bucket_name   The name of the S3 Bucket.
    key_name      The name of the object containing the data in S3.
    metadata      A Python dict object containing the new metadata.
                  For example: {'key1':'value1', 'key2':'value2'}
    """
    s3 = boto.connect_s3()
    bucket = s3.lookup(bucket_name)

    # Lookup the existing object in S3
    key = bucket.lookup(key_name)

    # Copy the key back on to itself, with new metadata
    key.copy(bucket.name, key.name, metadata, preserve_acl=True)

    return key
```

3.8 Find Out Who Is Accessing Your Data

Problem

You have content stored in S3 that is accessible to other people, and you would like to find out who is accessing it and when.

Solution

Use Server Access Logging to log access to your data.

Discussion

Server Access Logging can be enabled on any S3 bucket and will record information in log files each time data in the bucket is accessed. The log files themselves are also stored in an S3 bucket. You can store the logs in the same bucket you are logging or in another bucket, but the logged bucket and the destination bucket must be in the same S3 location.

Once logging is enabled, log files will start to appear in the logging destination bucket. You can specify a `prefix` string that will be prepended to all log file names to make it easier to identify specific logs.

 Logs are generated on a best-effort basis, so there is no guarantee that every access will be logged. If you require an absolute guarantee, you will need to devise a more deterministic approach.

Example 3-8. Enable Logging on an Existing Bucket

```python
import boto

def enable_logging(bucket_name,
                   log_bucket_name,
                   log_prefix=None):
    """
    Enable logging on a bucket.

    bucket_name     Bucket to be logged.
    log_bucket_name Bucket where logs will be written.
    log_prefix      A string which will be prepended to all log file names.
    """
    s3 = boto.connect_s3()
    bucket = s3.lookup(bucket_name)
    log_bucket = s3.lookup(log_bucket_name)

    # First configure log bucket as a log target.
    # This sets permissions on the bucket to allow S3 to write logs.
    log_bucket.set_as_logging_target()

    # Now enable logging on the bucket and tell S3
    # where to deliver the logs.
    bucket.enable_logging(log_bucket, target_prefix=log_prefix)

def disable_logging(bucket_name):
    """
    Disable logging on a bucket.

    bucket_name     Bucket that will no longer be logged.
    """
```

```
s3 = boto.connect_s3()
bucket = s3.lookup(bucket_name)
bucket.disable_logging()
```

3.9 Reduce the Cost of Storing Noncritical Data

Problem

You have large amounts of noncritical data stored in S3, and you would like to reduce
the cost of storage.

Solution

Use Reduced Redundancy Storage to reduce storage costs.

Discussion

S3 provides very durable data storage. In fact, by default, S3 provides 11 nines
(99.999999999%) of durability and can survive failures in two independent data cen-
ters. That's great to know, but if you are storing data that is transient or that is already
stored reliably elsewhere, you may not really need that level of durability.

Reduced Redundancy Storage (RRS) gives you the option to trade-off some of that
durability for reduced storage costs. For 33% less cost, you get 4 nines (99.99%) durability. If you are storing lots of this kind of data in S3, those savings can add up in a
hurry.

Example 3-9. Store an Object in S3 with RRS Storage Class

```
import boto
import os

def upload_file_rrs(local_file,
                    bucket_name,
                    key_name=None):
    """
    Upload a local file to S3 and store is using Reduced Redundancy Storage.

    local_file  Path to local file.
    bucket_name Bucket to which the file will be uploaded.
    key_name    Name of the new object in S3.  If not provided, the basename
                of the local file will be used.
    """
    s3 = boto.connect_s3()
    bucket = s3.lookup(bucket_name)

    # Expand common shell vars in filename.
    local_file = os.path.expanduser(local_file)
    local_file = os.path.expandvars(local_file)

    # If key_name was not provided, use basename of file.
```

```
    if not key_name:
        key_name = os.path.basename(local_file)

    # Create a new local key object.
    key = bucket.new_key(key_name)

    # Now upload file to S3
    key.set_contents_from_filename(local_file, reduced_redundancy=True)

def copy_object_to_rrs(bucket_name,
                       key_name):
    """
    Will change an existing standard storage class object to a
    Reduced Redundancy storage class object.

    bucket_name Bucket in which the existing key is located.
    key_name    Name of the existing, standard storage key.
    """
    s3 = boto.connect_s3()
    bucket = s3.lookup(bucket_name)
    key = bucket.lookup(key_name)

    return key.copy(bucket_name, key_name, reduced_redundancy=True,
                    preserve_acl=True)
```

3.10 Generating Expiring URLs for S3 Objects

Problem

You have private data that you would like to share with someone, but you don't want
to make it widely available.

Solution

Use Query String Authentication (QSA) to generate an expiring URL to your data in S3.

Discussion

One neat feature of S3 is the ability to generate self-expiring URLs pointing to data in
S3. This allows you to share private data in S3 without changing the permissions of the
object. It also means that you can control how long the URL you pass on to your
collaborator will work. You can have it expire in 5 seconds, 5 days, 5 months, or any
other time period that seems appropriate. The example below shows an interactive
session that creates a new, private object in S3, generates a URL that expires in 30
seconds, retrieves the object data, waits 30 seconds, and then attempts to retrieve the
data again to show that access is, in fact, denied.

Example 3-10. Generate an Expiring URL for an S3 Object

```
$ python
Python 2.7.1 (r271:86882M, Nov 30 2010, 10:35:34)
```

```
[GCC 4.2.1 (Apple Inc. build 5664)] on darwin
Type "help", "copyright", "credits" or "license" for more information.
>>> import boto, urllib2, time
>>> s3 = boto.connect_s3()
>>> b = s3.lookup('garnaat_pub')
>>> k = b.new_key('my_private_data_to_share.txt')
>>> k.set_contents_from_string('Python and AWS')
>>> url = k.generate_url(30)
>>> urllib2.urlopen(url).read()
'Python and AWS'
>>> time.sleep(30)
>>> urllib2.urlopen(url).read()
Traceback (most recent call last):
...
urllib2.HTTPError: HTTP Error 403: Forbidden
>>>
```

3.11 Preventing Accidental Deletion of Data from S3

Problem

You are using S3 as the primary storage location for critical data. You want to take precautions to make sure you don't accidentally delete the data.

Solution

Use Versioning and MFA Delete to protect your data in S3.

Discussion

As we mentioned before, S3 provides very durable data storage. But all that redundancy won't help if you accidentally delete data or if someone else maliciously deletes data. The S3 service provides two powerful tools to help you further protect your data:

Versioning

> Versioning means that you can have multiple objects within a bucket that all have the same name or key. This is possible because when versioning is enabled for a bucket, in addition to the name that you provide for an object, S3 also gives each object a unique version ID. With a version-enabled bucket, the simple DELETE operation cannot actually delete an object from your bucket. All it does is create a special delete marker in the bucket that shows the object was removed; you can still retrieve it by using its name and version ID. To actually delete an object, you need to perform a versioned DELETE operation that specifies both the object name and the version ID. This makes accidental deletion much less likely.

MFA Delete

> MFA (MultiFactor Authorization) Delete extends the protection of objects even further. Once MFA Delete is configured on a bucket, an object cannot be deleted without first providing an authentication token from a security device associated

with your account. This makes accidental deletion almost impossible and also means that someone who gains access to your AWS credentials still will be unable to delete your data unless they have also gained access to your physical security device.

For more information on MFA, see *http://aws.amazon.com/mfa/*

In this recipe, we will first show how to enable versioning on a bucket and how to access the version ID for objects within that bucket. Then we will show how to enable MFA Delete on a bucket and use the MFA device to actually perform a deletion.

Example 3-11. Enable Versioning on a Bucket

```
import boto

def configure_versioning(bucket_name, enable=True):
    """
    Enable versioning on a bucket.

    bucket_name  Bucket to be configured.
    enable       A boolean flag to indicate whether we are enabling
                 or disabling versioning for the bucket.
    """
    s3 = boto.connect_s3()
    bucket = s3.lookup(bucket_name)

    # Get the current status of versioning on the bucket
    # and print the value out.
    config = bucket.get_versioning_status()
    print 'Current Versioning Status: ', config

    # Now enable versioning on the bucket.
    bucket.configure_versioning(enable)

    # Update the status of versioning and print the new value.
    config = bucket.get_versioning_status()
    print 'New Versioning Status: ', config
```

Example 3-12. Enable MFA Delete on a Bucket

```
import boto

def configure_mfa_delete(bucket_name,
                         mfa_serial_number,
                         mfa_token,
                         enable=True):
    """
    Enable versioning on a bucket.

    bucket_name        Bucket to be configured.
    mfa_serial_number  The serial number of the MFA device associated
                       with your account.
    mfa_token          The current token displayed on the MFA device.
    enable             A boolean value to indicate whether MFA Delete
                       is being enabled or disabled.
```

```
"""
s3 = boto.connect_s3()
bucket = s3.lookup(bucket_name)

# Get the current status of versioning on the bucket
# and print the value out.
config = bucket.get_versioning_status()
print 'Current Versioning Status: ', config

if 'Versioning' in config and config['Versioning'] == 'Enabled':
    versioning = True
else:
    versioning = False

# Make change to configuration.  This method takes a tuple
# consisting of the mfa serial # and token.
bucket.configure_versioning(versioning=versioning, mfa_delete=enable,
                            (mfa_serial_number, mfa_token))

# Update the status of versioning and print the new value.
config = bucket.get_versioning_status()
print 'New Versioning Status: ', config
```

3.12 Hosting Static Websites on S3

Problem

You want to host a static website on S3.

Solution

Use the website configuration tools.

Discussion

In many ways, S3 seems like a perfect place to host a static website. There is virtually infinite storage capacity, fantastic bandwidth, high availability, and the ability to scale to handle lots of requests. So, why don't more people host websites on S3?

The main reason is that S3 did not provide support for automatically serving a default page (e.g., *index.html*) like a web server does, so you would have to count on your website visitors typing in the full path to the web page, or else they would be presented with a rather ugly and unfriendly XML page.

But that has all changed with the introduction of a new website feature in S3. Using this feature, you can upload the files for your website to an S3 bucket and then use a configuration command to tell S3 the name of the object in the bucket to use as the default page. You can also specify a custom error page in the same way.

This example defines an upload_website function that will automatically upload all of the files associated with your website from a local directory tree. It then configures the bucket and all files with the correct permissions and sets up the index and error files. Finally, it prints out the exact URL you can use to access your new website.

Example 3-13. Host a Website on S3

```
import boto
import os
import time

def upload_website(bucket_name,
                   website_dir,
                   index_file,
                   error_file=None):
    """
    Upload a static website contained in a local directory to
    a bucket in S3.

    bucket_name The name of the bucket to upload website to.
    website_dir Fully-qualified path to directory containing
                website.
    index_file  The name of the index file (e.g. index.html)
    error_file  The name of the error file.  If not provided
                the default S3 error page will be used.
    """
    s3 = boto.connect_s3()
    bucket = s3.lookup(bucket_name)

    # Make sure bucket is publicly readable
    bucket.set_canned_acl('public-read')

    for root, dirs, files in os.walk(website_dir):
        for file in files:
            full_path = os.path.join(root, file)
            rel_path = os.path.relpath(full_path, website_dir)
            print 'Uploading %s as %s' % (full_path, rel_path)
            key = bucket.new_key(rel_path)
            key.content_type = 'text/html'
            key.set_contents_from_filename(full_path, policy='public-read')

    # Now configure the website
    bucket.configure_website(index_file, error_file)

    # A short delay, just to let things become consistent.
    time.sleep(5)

    print 'You can access your website at:'
    print bucket.get_website_endpoint()
```

3.13 Uploading Large Objects to S3

Problem

You want to efficiently upload large objects to S3.

Solution

Use the MultiPart Upload feature.

Discussion

If you have large files to upload to S3, the new MultiPart (*http://aws.typepad.com/aws/ 2010/11/amazon-s3-multipart-upload.html*) feature of S3 is great. In the past, the only choice was to upload the entire file in one operation. If that operation failed on the very last byte of the file, you would have to start the whole process again. Now you can split the file up into as many chunks as you want and upload each chunk individually. If you have a failure with one chunk, it won't affect the others. When all of the chunks have been uploaded, you complete the operation and S3 then combines all of the chunks back into a single file. Because each chunk upload is a completely separate operation, it's also possible (and desirable) to use threads or processes to get several upload operations going concurrently to increase the overall throughput.

The easiest way to take advantage of this is to use the s3multiput utility that is installed as part of boto. This command-line utility handles all of the details for you. You just tell it where the input file is located and tell it what S3 bucket you want to store the file in, and it creates a set of subprocesses (based on the number of CPU cores you have) and gives each subprocess a list of chunks to upload. In the example below, the -c option tells the command to also print out some information that shows us the progress of each of the subprocesses:

```
% ls -l
...
-rw-r--r--  1 mitch  staff   265060652 Jun 21 08:45 mybigfile
...
$ s3multiput -b my_bucket -c 20 mybigfile
0 bytes transferred / 265060652 bytes total
0 bytes transferred / 265060652 bytes total
0 bytes transferred / 265060652 bytes total
0 bytes transferred / 265060652 bytes total
...
265060652 bytes tranferred / 265060652 bytes total
265060652 bytes tranferred / 265060652 bytes total
265060652 bytes tranferred / 265060652 bytes total
265060652 bytes tranferred / 265060652 bytes total
$
```

If you want to come up with your own custom code to handle MultiPart uploads, you can check out the source code for s3multipart as a good starting point.

About the Author

Mitch Garnaat is a software developer at Eucalyptus Systems, where he is responsible for the development of tools to make it easier to create and manage cloud computing resources. Previously, as a principal engineer at Xerox PARC, he was the co-inventor and lead developer of DocuShare, a web-based document management product from Xerox. He is the creator of boto, an open source Python library for cloud computing.

Get even more for your money.

Join the O'Reilly Community, and register the O'Reilly books you own. It's free, and you'll get:

- $4.99 ebook upgrade offer
- 40% upgrade offer on O'Reilly print books
- Membership discounts on books and events
- Free lifetime updates to ebooks and videos
- Multiple ebook formats, DRM FREE
- Participation in the O'Reilly community
- Newsletters
- Account management
- 100% Satisfaction Guarantee

Signing up is easy:

1. Go to: oreilly.com/go/register
2. Create an O'Reilly login.
3. Provide your address.
4. Register your books.

Note: English-language books only

To order books online:
oreilly.com/store

For questions about products or an order:
orders@oreilly.com

To sign up to get topic-specific email announcements and/or news about upcoming books, conferences, special offers, and new technologies:
elists@oreilly.com

For technical questions about book content:
booktech@oreilly.com

To submit new book proposals to our editors:
proposals@oreilly.com

O'Reilly books are available in multiple DRM-free ebook formats. For more information:
oreilly.com/ebooks

O'REILLY®

Spreading the knowledge of innovators   oreilly.com

The information you need, when and where you need it.

With Safari Books Online, you can:

Access the contents of thousands of technology and business books

- Quickly search over 7000 books and certification guides
- Download whole books or chapters in PDF format, at no extra cost, to print or read on the go
- Copy and paste code
- Save up to 35% on O'Reilly print books
- **New!** Access mobile-friendly books directly from cell phones and mobile devices

Stay up-to-date on emerging topics before the books are published

- Get on-demand access to evolving manuscripts.
- Interact directly with authors of upcoming books

Explore thousands of hours of video on technology and design topics

- Learn from expert video tutorials
- Watch and replay recorded conference sessions

CPSIA information can be obtained at www.ICGtesting.com
Printed in the USA
BVOW061118181112

305851BV00003B/1/P